I AM WITH
YOU STILL

Faith Reflections from
a Covid-19 World

VERITAS

Published 2021 by
Veritas Publications
7–8 Lower Abbey Street
Dublin 1, Ireland
publications@veritas.ie
www.veritas.ie

ISBN 978 1 84730 982 2

10 9 8 7 6 5 4 3 2 1

Compiled by Pamela McLoughlin
Design by Padraig McCormack
Printed in Ireland by SPRINT-print, Dublin

Veritas books are printed on paper made from the wood pulp of managed forests. For every tree felled, at least one tree is planted, thereby renewing natural resources.

Contents

Foreword

Donal Dorr

What an interesting idea: to invite eighteen people from very widely different backgrounds to share their reflections on finding God in the experience of living with Covid-19. And what a great variety of experiences they share with us. It seems to me that this is not a book to read straight through. It may be easier and more nourishing to dip in and out. If we do that, we'll find a chapter to suit each of our moods.

It is interesting to note that not only do the authors describe very different experiences but that they have very different ways of interpreting the request to write about experiencing God in the pandemic. Some respond by writing quite serious, reflective pieces about how best to survive this kind of lockdown, or about the important lessons we can learn in facing the future; these are written mostly by men. Others, written mostly by women, are far more experiential; they offer us moving accounts of how God has touched the author in the lockdown restrictions imposed by the pandemic or in the midst of bereavement.

Some of the contributions are written by people who have a deep involvement in Church ministry, including one by a Catholic bishop, one by a Presbyterian minister, and one by a priest working in a remote part of Africa. Others come out of quite different experiences – listening to the Muslim call to prayer in a deeply Islamic country, experiencing God on a journey by air back to Ireland, or finding God as one listens to music or in being visited by a robin.

There is an account of how Irish people have adapted to the limited numbers allowed to be present for a funeral: they now line up along the road as the hearse passes by. A very different kind of reflection comes from a Jewish person who links the experience of the pandemic with memories of being a child in a Nazi death-camp. Accompanying these chapters are shorter reflections from John Quinn, in which he shares joyful and sad memories from his time in lockdown and throughout his whole life.

In one way or another all of the contributions deal with finding that God is still relevant in their lives, as the title of the book suggests. But the kind of 'finding God' described here does not often involve a dramatic conversion. More often it is a keener awareness of the presence of God, or perhaps even just sensing something of the mystery within which we live out our lives.

It would make this preface unduly long if I were to refer here all of the different chapters in this book. So I suggest that you begin by sampling one or two of them. You may quickly find that this lures you into reading another one which turns out to be more interesting – and you may wonder why I didn't mention it here. In that case, when you buy a copy of the book for your friend, you can expand this preface, by adding your own recommendation of the chapters which you have found most interesting. But, in the meantime, do make sure that you read all of these diverse and thought-provoking accounts of how people have found that God is still with them in the midst of a pandemic.

Introduction

Pamela McLoughlin

There is no doubt that 2020 will long be remembered as a difficult year for us all. As the Covid-19 pandemic took hold of the world, people of all backgrounds, faiths, beliefs and ways of life were forced to come to terms with this new threat. People across the world were challenged physically, emotionally, financially and in some cases in their faith also as we adjusted to the 'new normal'.

For many, the past year has been an opportunity to look at the world with fresh eyes, to consider what is truly important in their lives and what changes needed to be made. For others, such as those who have lost loved ones or their livelihoods, this difficult time has raised many challenging questions, such as 'Why has this happened?' or 'Where can I find God in of all of this?'

Addressing the world from an empty St Peter's Square in Rome on Easter Sunday 2020, Pope Francis spoke to these concerns: '... the Lord has not left us alone! United in our prayer, we are convinced that he has laid his hand upon us, firmly reassuring us: Do not be afraid, "I have risen and I am with you still!"'

Our faith can play a big part in sustaining us in these hard times, in whatever form it may take. Many have found comfort in prayer or in the simple act of lighting a candle in a time of crisis or when they were thinking of someone. There is no doubt that many candles were lit throughout the world this last year for family, friends and essential workers in hopes that they would be safe, as well as for all who sadly lost their lives.

The idea behind this book was to give a voice to those who have faced some of these challenges and questions, that their experiences might help people come to terms with what they've been through and perhaps inspire them to look more deeply at what is important in their lives.

In compiling this book, I've been impressed and touched by the willingness of all of the contributors to speak, to express their fears, their frustrations and their vulnerabilities as they found their way through this crisis. Their words are testament to their faith and to their spirit and I thank each of them for their efforts. I would also like to give a special thanks to all involved in the production of this book: David Macken, Leeann Gallagher, Padraig McCormack and Colette Dower.

I hope you enjoy the stories, poems and reflections that follow and that they might offer you some comfort and hope as we look to the days ahead.

A Dream

A Reflection by John Quinn

And then one day
The fog of fear lifted
Gently
The night of anxiety passed
Quietly
And the pain of sickness and death eased
Palpably.
The seeds of faith
Found nourishment
In a warming sun.
The shoots of hope
Broke through
A frozen earth
And tender buds of love
Burst wildly open

On every branch.
The birds sang
With wild abandon
People laughed and danced
As was their right
And children played
Again.
Enmity and division
Were no more
And begrudgery
Withered away.

For on that bright and balmy morn
Faith wore its coat of many colours
Hope sang with the purest voice
And Love as always conquered all.

Where is God during the Pandemic?

Tomi Reichental

I came from a religious background. My grandfather, Jeckezkel Reichental, was deeply religious. I remembered him very well from at least the age of four. Every Friday we went to his home for the Sabbath dinner. We had to behave ourselves. Before the dinner began, he would pick up the prayer book and pray, finishing with the blessing to bring in the Sabbath. *'Baruch ata Adanoy elahenu Melech ha olam hamoutzi lechem min haretz.'* ('Blessed art thou, O Lord our God, King of the Universe who brings forth bread from the earth.')

From that moment on we were not allowed to do any work, run, drive, write, light a fire or switch on a light. It puzzled me. Where did God live? What would happen if I did any of these things which were prohibited on the Sabbath?

'Well,' my grandfather told me, 'God lives in heaven and he sees everyone. You cannot hide and if he catches you doing things which are not done on Sabbath, you will be punished.' He also told me that 'if you follow God's teachings, follow the Ten Commandments, going to Synagogue, observing the Sabbath, being an honest person and helping others – by keeping all of this, you will be rewarded in times of difficulty as God will look after you.'

I believed him. Not only was I afraid to do something against God's wishes, but I would tell others when I saw them doing something that was prohibited, 'God will punish you!' For a long time, I thought God was in heaven sitting on a large gilded throne, with a long beard, looking at us and making sure we were good, and that he loved people who were following his teaching.

As I was growing up, I also began to understand the difference between good and evil. I realised, that amongst good people there were many dishonest evil people who were not punished.

When I was six years old strangers in uniform came to my grandfather's shop and told him, under the new rules and regulations by the government, as a Jew his shop would be confiscated and locked down. Not only had he lost his livelihood but also his spirit to live. In July 1942, he and my grandmother, Katarina, were arrested, taken away and we never saw them again. They were murdered in Auschwitz.

As I became older I began my education in the local school. Very soon after starting my first class, however, I was expelled from the school. Why? Because I was a Jew! Not long after, when I encountered kids on the street, they were shouting at me, 'You dirty Jew'. Life became restricted and I began to understand that the Jewish people were being persecuted by the government with harsher and harsher restrictive laws. Daily, we were receiving information that many family members and friends were being arrested. I remember at the time my mother and father speaking Hungarian in a whisper in front of my brother and I so that we would not understand what they were saying. It was all bad news; they did not want to let us know and frighten us.

It was during this time at the beginning of 1942 that many of my relatives were taken away. We said 'goodbye' to them, hoping that when all of this was over, we would be reunited and that it was only a bad dream. But, unfortunately, we never saw them again. They were all murdered in the extermination camps. I lost thirty members of my family at this time: uncles, aunts, cousins and grandparents.

I was seven years old when I began to think for the first time about what my grandfather had taught me about God. We were good people. I had never harmed anyone. Why did other children hate me? Why were we being punished? I followed God's teaching! I followed the ten commandments! We the Jewish people were being persecuted, arrested, sent to working camps and extermination camps. We had to hide to avoid arrest and we were living in constant fear of being betrayed. I remember what my grandfather told me – 'God will look after you' – but it only got worse. Finally, at the end of 1944 we were betrayed, taken away, dumped in a cattle cart and deported to Bergen-Belsen concentration camp.

I was now nine years old and what greeted us in Bergen-Belsen concentration camp was hell on earth. We were living amongst skeletons walking around aimlessly and occasionally falling down never to get up again. The situation was becoming worse with passing time. We are starving, freezing and watching the people around us succumb to the progression of starvation, disease and death. Inmates are dying in vast numbers. The corpses are in piles being placed all around us. As children, where can we play? The only place is among the piles of corpses.

The question 'Where is God?' became louder and louder.

We were liberated on 15 April 1945. I was ten years old. I survived the Holocaust, the most cataclysmic event in human history. I was not the only one asking the question 'Where was God?' and I am still asking the question today.

Of course my experiences have influenced my thoughts and attitude towards religion. Can I totally dismiss the existence of God? In a sense, the question of 'Where is God during the Covid-19 pandemic?' is not new to me.

A long time has passed since my belief as a child that there is a man with a long beard sitting in a gilded throne in heaven called God. The question still remains: what or who is God? Unless one is a theologian or a philosopher, we will have a great difficulty explaining the existence of God, but most of humanity believes in this supreme being which we worship and call God.

Whether we ask 'Where was God during the Holocaust?' or 'Where is God during the Covid-19 pandemic?' or any other tragic event, all events are human tragedies and no miracle occurred that we could ascribe to the hand of God stopping the hardship and deaths from happening.

I was searching for some answers or interpretation in simple terms of what makes us believe in God. Let us mention some philosophical or theologian perspectives in light of terrible events such as the Holocaust and the lack of intervention on God's part:

- It is the price we have to pay for having free will. God will not and cannot interfere with history, otherwise our free will would effectively cease to exist. Eliezer Berkovits, for example, stressed that God is all powerful but that he curtails his own freedom to respect human freedom, even with such horrific consequences.[1]

- Life is a mystery. It contains blessings and tragedies, joy and pain, light and darkness. Just because we are unable to sense God's manifestation in the darkness, should not lead us to dismiss his presence in times of illumination.

- Talk of God's care can be in pastoral terms rather than practical ones. People may endure hardship but still feel loved by God, and that sense of relationship helps them to carry on, rather than give up in despair.

- We humans, with our limited minds, cannot expect to understand God's ways. We must live with faith despite our unanswered questions.
- A quote on the wall of a prison cell in Mauthausen concentration camp was inscribed with: 'If there is a God, he will have to beg for my forgiveness!'
- Finally, we must also consider: 'God did not create man, man created God'.

Coming back to our original question: Where is God during the pandemic? I hope the genius of the human race will find the solution and we will overcome this natural disaster and tragedy, rather than waiting for a miracle for the pandemic to disappear.

Going back to my grandfather's teachings and the teachings of God (though not necessarily the religious parts), I strived to be fair, honest, and helpful to others all my life. Was I rewarded as my grandfather promised? I think so!

I belong to a small minority that survived, against all odds, the most unimaginable tragedy and genocide in human history. Years later, I participated in a war on the frontline to protect our survival. In later years, I had a life-threatening operation and survived again. Is it all just good luck? Perhaps. But I have had a good life. Maybe there is somebody looking after me!

ENDNOTES

1   Eliezer Berkovits, *Faith after the Holocaust*, New York: KTAV Publishing House, 1973.

First Night

A Reflection by John Quinn

The fifth of September 1954. First night in Ballyfin, a boarding school for boys. First night away from home. Sixty miles away from home. A large dormitory with fifty beds. Strange faces, strange voices. Starched clean sheets with my name sewn on them. Lights out. A fearful silence. An occasional stifled whimper. Please let sleep come.

Bright early morning. Brother Angelus marches through the dormitory, ringing a handbell. Beginning of a strange routine. Clamour for a handbasin. Cold, cold water. The towel smells of home. My brother tells me to hurry up. Good to have a brother here. Down the stone stairs to Mass in the oratory. I am not here.

I wish I were at home. Mammy gone to Mass to pray for me. Daddy stoking the range. Roy, our dog awaiting release from his kennel. I am fearful, confused about the day ahead. The pain will ease slowly. Friends will be made. Roll on Christmas – 'Fifty-six days to go ...' we will write in our copybooks. Roll on the next five years. We will survive. Everything passes ... All will be well. All will be well.

One Flock, One Shepherd

✠ Fintan Monahan

An editorial in *The Tablet* early last year voiced
the opinion that, as the Covid-19 pandemic is
not anywhere near over, now is not the time to
consider its implications for parish life. It went
on to suggest that the Vatican might have been
premature in publishing that week a document
on reform of parish life.[1]

One can see the value of biding time and not
rushing to draw lessons from the pandemic as it
still rages throughout the world but at the same
time it is good to see the Church considering
reform in parish life. The big questions I see facing
the Church at this time and which must be among
the first to be answered (or at least considered)
are: do we return to a model of parish that we

had in pre-Covid-19 times, or do we devise a new model of Church in the parish?

It has almost become the mantra of these hurting times that there will be 'no going back' and that a 'terrible beauty' lies ahead in what is deemed the 'new normal'. Is it wise for the Church to change its parish model on the dictate of the virus? There would be an element of prematurity also in allowing the virus to set the pace for reform just as it seems to be setting the pace for everything in society just now in the struggle to overcome it. Perhaps, we should name the reality differently and suggest that Covid-19's lockdowns and standstills have given us time to reflect more on the need for change, a need that was already with us prior to the virus.

There is no doubt that during the days of lockdown we were given insights into the communication capabilities of the local Church, which in some cases were considerably lacking while others were 'in touch' through various forms of media outreach long before that. The lockdown caused many parishes to catch up very quickly and it will be very unusual in the future to find a parish not utilising modern technology to bring God's Word into people's homes.

It is one thing to have the medium in place to transmit the message, but the question as to how well we present the message will need to be assessed. Will Mass over a webcam continue to be the only offering and will it remain the flat impersonal narrow reproduction of altar-based activity that some people found uninspiring and boring, as was previously the main public criticism of our Eucharistic celebrations?

We are still journeying through the pandemic. The emphasis is still on personal and public safety and the state of our future remains unclear. It is too soon for the Church to draw conclusions about its future direction. Right now, we need to be calm in our approach and accepting that there will be a mixed bag of relative success and failure in our attempts to eventually emerge from this time of crisis as a Church which has learned and is prepared to implement lessons about its parish model of Church.

There seems to be common acceptance of the prospects of a 'new normal'. However, we should not underestimate the reluctance of people to change in any dramatic way. It would not surprise me (depending on the duration of the virus) that people will make every effort in time to restore things to the way they were before the Covid-19 pandemic. One can almost hear voices of disagreement shout back that 'no way is that going to happen!' The world changes slowly and two world wars, nuclear threats, a miscellaneous array of things like the Cuban Missile Crisis, AIDS virus, Millennium Bug, Foot and Mouth, Swine Flu, Ebola and Bird Flu have all hit the world in the past and were life-changing experiences. Yet, the change from all of these was not necessarily overnight but was an evolving and often more subtle change than people had imagined would take place. Humanity has an instinct to restore order and I feel that for the Church to pin any hope for reform or change on the effects of the Covid-19 crisis alone could be disappointing in the results.

To borrow and slightly tweak Dickens' line, one might say that the Covid-19 crisis is the worst of times. However, the time of reflection provided by lockdown might make it the best of times too. This brings me to an important point for us bishops, priests, and lay Church ministers and that is the need now for a gentler language in our dealing with one another. I sometimes sense that the language of the gospel, which is the language of love, has been missing from our reaction to the pandemic. We as a Church have been as shocked as anyone at the arrival of the virus and, like many, we have been recovering from the shock ever since. In both closing and re-opening our churches we (correctly) acted according to a set of rules that reflected a very functional response. We are good at functionality but at times we are weak at responding in a human and more understanding way. Hence, we speak in directives and adopt an official advisory tone which no matter how correct and well intentioned can come over as cold and detached.

I am certain that there were times and there will continue to be times when people need a gentler and warmer voice – the voice of love. The Covid-19 pandemic has hit our First World country and our First World Church in a manner many of us have not been accustomed to in our lifetime. Such health crises we have regarded as only occurring in poorer countries, but this virus is rampant and spreads everywhere and, of course, the poorer countries still suffer the most from it. I think we are all shocked at this new reality that our prosperous and forward-thinking country can be so hurt and incapacitated by this virus. To help us cope with the now and the immediate future we as faithful Church members need to comfort one another with the message of Christ and the riches of our faith.

It is a great challenge as to how we do this. I cannot honestly suggest a clear pathway for change or practical guidelines we should implement for renewal of Church life as we face the future. It will require far more reflection than I have given it to date. However, some things that we should not do are clearer and by not doing them we might see our way to doing what would be more right.

- It is not a time to fall back on pious platitudes and hollow words of comfort – it is more honest to acknowledge our fears and our uncertainties in facing this crisis.

- It is not a time to encourage blind faith or blind trust in God – our faith is always shaken by crises in our lives and it is a time now to pray for a strengthening and deepening of personal faith.

- As a Church concerned with falling numbers in pre-Covid-19 times, we must not be opportunistic and view the crisis as a moment of return to God – no, it is not so much that we should be hoping for an increase in numbers coming back to their faith or the Church, but as a time to be reaching out and going out of our Church's comfort zones to be with one another at this time.

- It is not a time to circle wagons of faith and delude ourselves into thinking that this is the early onset of and return to basic Christian communities – if anything it is a time when we are being forced to realise that the day of the Church as being a strong institution as well as finding its local identity around the physical church building might be over.

- It is not a time to hold fast to old ways and refuse to learn anything new from the crisis by insisting we get back to the way things were in the Church – we must learn to let go of some mores that we mistook for healthy faith-living. Our countryside is dotted with ruined churches and monasteries; old ways gave way to new and it was painful back then and it will be painful now too. The Covid-19 pandemic is teaching us the hard lesson of our scripture: that in it, as in dying, we are born again.

- The Covid-19 pandemic is not the *Apocalypse Now* of our time – our preaching must be hopeful and not burdened with declaiming messages of woe. Whether we speak God's word from the pulpit or over social media we must not abuse any such medium by even a tiny hint that this experience of this pandemic is God punishing his people.

Human nature being what it is, we have brought a fight or flight approach to our coping with the pandemic. We are eternally grateful to frontline workers who are continuing to fight on our behalf. Many people have reacted in flight mode by isolating themselves according to HSE guidelines and this is a good thing for as long as we are asked to behave in this way. Some have been so gripped by fear that they have extended the public lockdown to a worrying new sphere of personal lockdown.

Sadly, there are those who do not think it their obligation to accept any form of responsibility for the common good and they have disrespected most forms of protection as advised by the health experts. I wonder if it is not a case of their being unable to deal with painful reality and that they have gone into a form of denial. The temptation is to judge them in a harsh light, but I feel the better approach is to keep channels of communication open and to reinforce the model of best practice at every opportunity.

It is early days yet and the future is uncertain. Change will be a gradual thing as we come in time to decipher any lessons to be learned from this crisis. We might begin to build on the two early lessons that lockdown taught us: people's openness to reach out to one another in a manner that spoke of Christianity in action and the opportunity for personal reflection it gave all of us. We have lived for a long time with the Vatican II view that the Church is the people of God. There is no better time than now to harness the potential of good in the collective *pobal Dé* of our Church. Those of us in leadership as priests or bishops might rethink our approach to leadership and reflect more on the notion of following the lead we see being given by our lay sisters and brothers at this time. It would be very scriptural in the sense of the Good Shepherd mirroring the action of the shepherd in Christ's time who followed their flocks.

It may be that we have laboured over Pope Francis' line exhorting us to live with the smell of the sheep; but its relevance cannot be overlooked at this point of realising a new solidarity with our co-disciples. If the Church has any purpose in today's world it is its original purpose of spreading the good news of God's kingdom on earth. Our ways and means of doing so change with the times and the current times are calling us to be a spiritual presence in the world. It will require courage and humility to be the spiritual voice in today's world, but it is again a scripture-oriented calling: 'the voice of one crying in the wilderness: "Prepare the way of the Lord"'(Is 40:3). The Church is called to be a prophetic witness today, but it may take us time to understand how best to be prophets. The current pandemic may be our long road to Emmaus in the company of a Christ whom we only partly recognise. We look forward in hope to the day when our eyes will be opened and we will fully recognise Christ.

ENDNOTES

1   'Parish Life but Not as We Know It', *The Tablet*, 23 July 2020.
    https://www.thetablet.co.uk/editors-desk/1/18452/parish-life-
    but-not-as-we-know-it; accessed on 1 January 2021.

Skellig

A Reflection by John Quinn

Of all the places I have visited, my outright favourite is the Great Skellig Rock off the Kerry coast. I made a radio documentary there in September 2000 and I was privileged to spend a night there. Such a unique and sacred place. Home to monks for centuries, living in their cillíns – a life of prayer and penury, sacrifice and isolation. A wild and fearful place in winter. Bitterly cold. Violent storms. Largely a barren rock, but these holy men lived off what land and sea offered. And they lived their entire monastic lives there. No luxuries. No contact with the world beyond. Alone.

But they *wanted* to be there. Far from the world, but near to their God. An early example of self-isolation. In these days, may we capture something of their spirit, their courage, their trust in their God.

'There is a time for everything'[1]

Anne Neylon DC

THE EXPERIENCE OF COVID-19

Saint John Henry Newman said, 'To live is to change, and to be perfect is to have changed often.'[2] Change was immediate in the initial experience of Covid-19. A sudden lockdown descended, graphically described by Br. Richard Hendrick in his poem 'Lockdown'.[3] Worldwide news broadcasts and social media brought frightening news of daily rising death tolls due to the coronavirus. The rapid and swift responses of the government, the authorities and primarily the prompt, compassionate, professional and self-sacrificing efforts of frontline workers revealed that the country was in as far as possible safe hands. Love and care abounded.

Day by day, the authorities imposed restrictions; slogans were repeated like mantras; 'Stay Safe. Stay at Home. Save Lives.' A new language and lifestyle emerged as people washed their hands and maintained social distance. Losses were many, as loved ones died in lonely circumstances. Funerals were difficult with stringent restrictions. Schools closed and school principals and their staff quickly adapted to online teaching, with roles stretched to regular house-to-house visitations distributing lunches, iPads and textbooks. Working parents juggled their lives as they multitasked with 'work from home', blended learning, childcare, entertaining their children and housekeeping! No longer were grandparents available to mind the children. What a shock! To recall the words of Friedrich Neitzsche, 'He who has a *why* to live for can bear with almost any *how*.'[4]

Challenges disrupted families to varying degrees. Lack of space, crowded conditions, home-schooling, social distancing, addictions, poverty and restrictions on social life caused anxiety. Levels of domestic abuse increased and, for many, the disruption of the routine of daily life presented trouble. Change was constant and inevitable.

> … Made weak by time and fate, but strong in will, to strive, to seek, to find, and not to yield.[5]

Tennyson describes being weakened by 'time and fate'. In weakness, the Christian is strong (2 Cor 12:10). The prophets Isaiah (1:2–4), Jeremiah (26:1–6) and Amos (3:1–2) called God's people to conversion but they didn't listen. Consequently, they suffered in exile but they returned in God's time. God never forgets the covenant with his people. Jesus' teaches the disciples to stay awake and be ready (Mt 24:42–44). 'Ready for what?' I thought. Jesus' promise to be with us always offers assurance. Pope Francis' constantly calls people to hear the cry of the poor and the cries of an ailing planet.

The calls are louder than the responses society ever made.

Greta Thunberg's sharp words resonated within me, 'You have stolen my dreams and my childhood with your empty words. And yet I'm one of the lucky ones. People are suffering. People are dying. Entire ecosystems are collapsing.'[6]

God's gentle, persistent call to trust remains stronger than other voices. God speaks, 'Behold I am coming to do a new thing' (Is 43:19); 'I have loved you with and everlasting love' (Jer 31:3).

Time passes and hope and joy are steadfast. The world lives with the coronavirus. The country's top priority is to open schools for the new academic year. Gallant efforts are in progress to prepare for the new normal. In a letter, Leonardo DeLorenzo wrote, 'Dear Students: There is no Afterwards'.[7] In it, though he acknowledges the suffering caused by the Covid-19 pandemic, he considers if there might be 'a gift' in it as well. DeLorenzo advises his students 'to respond to the given circumstances with humility and courage'.[8]

Hope is alive, as scripture proclaims. Just as Jacob woke from sleep and said, 'Surely the Lord is in this place, and I did not know it' (Gn 28:16), we also are invited to believe in God's powerful and imminent presence. It seems God is setting his people on a journey during the Covid-19 pandemic, accompanying them as a pillar of cloud by day and a pillar of fire by night (Ex 13:21).

Prayer is essential for this journey and from the outset Pope Francis called people to pray. He set out a calendar for the world to pray in solidarity. From March 2020, Pope Francis celebrated daily Mass, which was accessible online, from his residence in Casa Santa Marta, Rome. Pope Francis introduced St Alphonsus Ligouri's 'Spiritual Prayer of Communion' recited at each celebration of the Eucharist.

One of the most poignant moments of prayer was held in Rome on 27 March 2020 when Pope Francis officiated at the 'Extraordinary Moment of Prayer' and gave the *Urbi et Orbi* special blessing. The memory lingers of Pope Francis standing in silence in prayer at the foot of the miraculous crucifix and at the icon of Our Lady, *Salus Populi Romani*. This crucifix and icon held a special place in the Sagrato of St Peter's Basilica for this momentous occasion. In former times, both crucifix and icon venerated in prayer protected the city of Rome from plague. Pope Francis encouraged listeners to 'get our lives back on track' and to reawaken to God, knowing and believing 'that nothing can separate them from the love of Christ'.[9]

The use of technology has enhanced daily lives during lockdown. Some began to laud the idea of 'working from home', acknowledging the use of Zoom as economical, convenient, and time and environmentally friendly. The authorities prompted people to use creative ways to communicate. A kind gesture from An Post provided free postcards to send by free post.

Opportunity arose during the Covid-19 pandemic to reflect earnestly on Pope Francis' Encyclical Letter, *Laudato Si'*. In addition, a new book, *Theology and Ecology in Dialogue: The Wisdom of Laudato Si'*, launched in June 2020 via webinar, encourages readers to a deeper understanding of how 'ecological questions should permeate the whole area of theology'.[10] This timely moment enables people to internalise Pope Francis' thoughts from the first chapter of *Laudato Si'*, 'What is happening to our Common Home'.[11]

Initially, given the two-kilometre allowance for daily exercise, there was much to observe and discover about our local common home in the beautiful parks of the Gaels, Glenaulin Park and the California Hills of Ballyfermot. The fresh air, sunshine and beauty of late spring and early summer are etched in my heart and mind. Families benefitted greatly from the wide open spaces and the green fields. People walked their dogs regularly and rumour had it that there wasn't a dog or a bicycle for sale in Ballyfermot! Trees and shrubs circulated invigorating scents. I met many people who shared their hopes and joys at a social distance. Many discovered a new vision for their lives. The words of Blessed Rosalie Rendu DC rang in my ears. As she walked with

God, she said, 'Never have I prayed so well as in the streets.'[12]

God invited us personally and communally to an enhanced community life as Daughters of Charity, given to God, in community, to serve the poor during the Covid-19 pandemic. Prayer was truly at the heart of each day. Ministries continued with a different shape and momentum. Keeping social distance and maintaining the restrictions in our lifestyle brought their own challenges. Pope Francis offered wise advice when he said, 'Prayer and quiet service: these are our victorious weapons.'[13] Powerful words!

The local parish church, Our Lady of Assumption, Ballyfermot, was a refuge for parishioners. The celebration of Eucharist took place daily behind closed doors via webcam. After Mass, in adhering to all rules and regulations, the church opened for private prayer. People who lived within the two-kilometre limit and within the age range faithfully visited each day and lit candles at the various shrines. The church was a haven of peace as the atmosphere of prayer was sustained with background music and meditative images on the screens.

People evaluated time in the midst of the pandemic in different ways. Some felt the time as being long and were upset about the closure of pubs, gyms, cinemas, theatres and nightclubs. Others cried bitterly because of their loved ones in hospital with Covid-19. They prayed and pleaded with God for help. Thankfully many people recovered, but many died. Still others saw it as a time of fruition and some said without their own spark of faith, they wouldn't have survived.

ABOUT THE FUTURE

The future is unfolding and there is no going back to pre-Covid-19 times. The world has moved on. The Church is in a new place and God is creating anew. Saint John affirms, 'God is love' (1 Jn 4:16), and St Vincent de Paul said, 'Love is inventive to infinity'.[14]

In line with former popes, Pope Francis urges 'the pastoral conversion of the parish community.'[15] He urges 'creativity' and prompts the Church to plumb the depths of 'innumerable possibilities' to seek new ways to proclaim the gospel.[16] The pope advocates that the Church be an attractive place for all. He hopes that God's people 'will be moved by the fear of remaining shut up within structures which give us a false sense of security, within rules which make us harsh judges, within habits which make us feel safe, while at our door people are starving and Jesus does not tire of saying to us: "Give them something to eat" (Mk 6:37).'[17]

Pope Saint John Paul II identified parish as 'an indispensable organism of primary importance in the visible structure of the Church'. He recognised 'evangelisation as the cornerstone of all pastoral action.' The demands of evangelisation are 'primary, preeminent and preferential'.[18]

Benedict XVI described the parish as 'a beacon that radiates the light of the faith and thus responds to the deepest and truest desires of the human heart, giving meaning and hope to the lives of individuals and families'.[19] Pope Francis expresses the role of parish as one which 'encourages and trains its members to be evangelisers'.[20]

The vital question for this time is: How can the parish encourage and train its members to be evangelisers? A practical vision for the parish is critical. Its implementation is equally critical. God instructed the prophet Habakkuk to write the vision down (Hab 2:1–3). The vital necessity of having a vision is written in Proverbs, 'Without a vision, the people perish' (Prov 29:18).

Throughout history, visions are scribed. In his book *A New Century Dawns*, Robert Maloney CM set a vision for the future of the Church, including that of the Vincentian Family.[21] Maloney takes Priscilla and Aquila in the New Testament and writes about their importance in the Church of their time. He explores what can be gleaned about Priscilla and Aquila in the various texts of the Bible. He asks a challenging question: 'Will the role of lay Catholics continue to be revitalised in the twenty-first century?' Then he expresses his hopes for 'lay women and men' in the future Church.[22]

The National Directory, *Share the Good News* (2010), provides a framework for 'evangelisation, catechesis and religious education today, and motivating us to study and research all the means to bring the gospel to life anew every day'.[23] This fine document still holds much potential.

Let us return to Pope Francis' familiar question: 'What kind of world do we want to leave to those who come after us, to children who are now growing up?'[24] Let's be bold and courageous as we seek and respond to God's will.

ENDNOTES

1   Ecclesiastes 3:1.

2   John Henry Newman, An Essay on the Development of Christian Doctrine, London: James Toovey, 1845, p. 39.

3   Richard Hendrick OFM Cap 'Lockdown', Facebook post dated 13 March 2020.

4   Quoted in Victor, E Frankl, 'Man's Search For Meaning' (Trans. I. Lasch), Boston: Beacon Press, 2014, p. 72.

5   Alfred Lord Tennyson, 'Ulysses', *The Works of Alfred Tennyson, Poet Laureate*, London: P.C. Kegan, 1985.

6   Greta Thunberg's Speech at the U.N. Climate Action Summit, 23 September 2019.

7   Leonardo DeLorenzo, 'Dear Students, There Is No Afterwards', *Church Life Journal*, 25 March 2020. https://churchlifejournal. nd.edu/articles/dear-students-there-is-no-afterwards/; accessed on 1 January 2021.

8   Ibid.

9   Pope Francis, Extraordinary Moment of Prayer, Sagrato of St Peter's Basilica, 27 March 2020. www.vatican.va/ content/francesco/en/homilies/2020/documents/papa-francesco_20200327_omelia-epidemia.html; accessed on 1 January 2021.

10   Dermot A. Lane, *Theology and Ecology in Dialogue: The Wisdom of Laudato Si'*, Dublin: Messenger Publications, 2020.

11   Pope Francis, *Laudato Si'*, Rome: Libreria Editrice Vaticana, 2015.

12   Rosalie Rendu (1786-1856). http://www.vatican.va/news_ services/liturgy/saints/ns_lit_doc_20031109_rendu_en.html; accessed on 1 January 2021.

13   Pope Francis, Extraordinary Moment of Prayer.

14 Vincent De Paul, *Correspondence, Conferences, Documents*, (M. Poole, Ed.) Vol. 9, New York: New City Press, 1995, p. 67.

15 Instruction 'The Pastoral Conversion of the Parish Community in the Service of the Evangelising Mission of the Church', of the Congregation for the Clergy, 27 June 2020. http://press.vatican.va/content/salastampa/en/bollettino/pubblico/2020/07/20/200720a.html; accessed on 1 January 2021.

16 Ibid., 1.

17 Ibid., 3.

18 Ibid., 12.

19 Ibid., 12.

20 Ibid., 12.

21 Robert P. Maloney, *A New Century Dawns: Hopes for the Vincentian Family*, www.svdpusa.org, pp. 42–7.

22 Ibid. pp. 43–7.

23 Irish Episcopal Conference, *Share the Good News: National Directory for Catechesis in Ireland*, Dublin: Veritas Publications, 2010.

24 *Laudato Si'*, 160.

An Easter Prayer

A Reflection by John Quinn

In selfless devotion and care
In our willingness to share
   Christ our Redeemer is risen, Alleluia
In our anxiety and our deepest fears
In our suffering and our tears
   Christ our Redeemer is risen, Alleluia
In the cheer of birds that sing
In the welcome growth of spring
   Christ our Redeemer is risen, Alleluia
In a world where we've learned to be kind
And where love has been redefined
   Christ our Redeemer is risen, Alleluia
In our hopes that present sorrow
Will give way to a brighter morrow
   Christ our Redeemer is risen, Alleluia

In our silence and reflection
In all our cherished connection
    Christ our Redeemer is risen, Alleluia
In a time when all's changed in our world
And a whole new future will be unfurled
    Christ our Redeemer is risen, Alleluia

Pandemic 2020: An Intergenerational Family's Journey

John and Nancy DeStefano

Our life-journey is replete with many tests. Here in the USA both the Covid-19 pandemic (now coupled with annual flu assault) and our national 2020 political endemic provide unprecedented challenges. Responding to these tests and challenges is a chapter of our 'faith-life' story. Reflecting on the story of Jesus, and the people of God of both the Old Covenant and the New Covenant gives us insight that guides our response.

Our home is an intergenerational family home in Celina, Texas – a small but growing town about forty miles north of Dallas. We live with the family of one of our three children, Megan, her husband Marcus, and three of our five grandchildren, Mallory, Matthew and Madelynne. Our dog, Fritz; their three dogs, Sammy, Toby, and Max; and their two cats, Miranda and Meredith, add a 'visit-to-the-zoo-like' dimension to our continuing now nine-month isolation.

Our three children Katie, Megan, and Kevin grew in their concern with the safety of our living together with Megan and her family. 'Should we remain living with Megan and her family?' 'Would renting an apartment close to Megan and her family be the better option?' They shared their discussions with us. We were adamant we remain living where we were and make some adaptations to our room and turn it into a mini-apartment-like room. What was a bathroom is now bathroom-kitchen with a refrigerator in our closing closet; and the linen closet, a food pantry; and the shower and sink area, a cooking area with a microwave, grill, toaster oven, and a Keurig coffee maker. Oops, almost forgot! The sinks are now washing machines powered by human hands.

The first phase of Covid-19 included stay-at-home quarantine for everyone. Our homelife now began to change. Megan and Marcus and I (Nancy) worked from home, which we continue to do today. The kitchen and dining room tables became a two-room schoolhouse with Nancy as principal and teacher. Megan and Marcus did and continue to do the in-store shopping. Our front porch, for better or worse, has become an Amazon drop-off site.

Covid-19 had minimal negative impact on our town of Celina. Local government began to loosen quarantine and isolation by June. Megan and her family began to interact socially with two neighboring families. This gave the grandchildren opportunity to play outdoors with three of their friends, providing them (and their parents) with some relief from being 'locked up'. Our grandchildren also began limited participation in athletics. This, in turn, changed the manner of our interaction with them. Imagine the test and challenge that limiting their physical presence has been for us.

It often felt as if we were now on this journey alone and isolated. Matthew was quarantined from school for ten days when a friend tested positive. Mallory had developed Covid-19-like symptoms but tested negative. The house became silent with the absence of the sounds of the laughter and sibling fighting. Sharing time, storytelling and hugging daily soon faded. We no longer ate meals together.

Our other children, Katie and Kevin, are both teachers and coaches. They interact daily face-to-face with students and athletes and have been in the presence students and athletes who tested positive. The possibility of their carrying the virus without knowing it and passing it on to us is another bump on the road that is testing our living skills. The absence of their face-to-face presence weighs heavily on us.

Presence is one of life's most cherished gifts. Grief, in some form, always accompanies the loss of the presence of a family member even when that loss is for a brief time. Our isolation during the pandemic has deepened our understanding of the precious gift of presence. We now 'enjoy' the presence of our family who live in Conway, Arkansas, and Austin, Texas, virtually on FaceTime, Zoom and daily phone calls. Once skeptical of 'virtual presence', we are growing to appreciate it as a form of 'real' presence. Our presence with one another need not be limited to physical presence.

Zoom and FaceTime have been effectual means of face-to-face conversation with others. These times together have enabled me (Nancy) to continue my responsibilities as pastoral ministry. Here are three examples:

- Weekly Zoom face-to-face conversations with members of the Church in the second half of their life. During these conversations we share past and present experiences that are part our life-faith stories.
- Monthly Zoom conversations with the Stephen Ministers. These conversations support their one-to-one care to members of

the Church who are experiencing a difficult time in their life.

- Pastoral counselling and spiritual direction via FaceTime, Zoom, or iPhone conversations.

The human journey is more than a life journey. Christians believe life on earth is a 'faith-life' journey rooted in hope and love. God tells us we are now on a journey of deliverance from brokenness to wholeness, a journey of deliverance to the new Creation, to the kingdom of God where we will respond to the reign of God and live the Great Commandments to their fullness.

The pandemic is giving us pause to value living in the present and in the presence of God. Yesterday's leg of our journey is *past*; tomorrow is yet to come, the unknown *future*; the *present* is all that is. Yes, remembering how we lived our past is important. Yes, knowing how our past has and continues to impact our present is vital. Perhaps, most importantly, it is how we live in the present keeps us on the road to the kingdom and makes us co-creators with God of the new Creation in Christ.

Faith is God's invitation to know that the Trinity, our unseen God, does not simply watch us from above as we walk our journey. God is present with us every nano-second of our life. God's Word is a never-ending invitation to trust in the divine, ever-present God. God is always with us, celebrating with us, grieving with us, healing our brokenness, and transforming our hardened hearts with divine life and love to join with Jesus Christ in working to build the kingdom, the new Creation, announced and inaugurated in him.

A final reflection. The Exodus story is the epic story of the human journey of deliverance. From a burning bush God announces he will deliver the Israelites from slavery and informs Moses that God has chosen him to lead the people on that journey. Moses hears a voice saying, 'I am the God of your father, the God of Abraham, the God of Isaac, and the God of Jacob.' Moses asks God, 'If I come to the Israelites and say to them, "The God of your ancestors has sent me to you," and they ask me, "What is his name?" what shall I say to them?' God said to Moses, 'I Am Who I Am … I Am has sent me to you' (Ex 3:13–14). We have come to understand God reaffirming, 'I always Am; I Am always present with you.' God continued this divine reaffirmation in the gospel, saying, '"Look a virgin shall conceive and bear a son, and they shall name him Emmanuel," which means, "God is with us"' (Mt 1:23). And before the Ascension the risen Jesus' last words to the disciples and to all were, 'I am with you always, to the end of the age' (Mt 28:20). We are still navigating the stormy waters of the pandemic and, in the USA, a toxic political and social endemic. Listening to the account of the disciples' response to the storm and raging waters in Mark 4:35–41, we take heart. We also take to heart the writer of Hebrews to the Christians being persecuted in Rome, 'Exhort one another every day, as long as it is called "today," so that none of you may be hardened by the deceit' (Heb 3:13).

Dandelions and Me

A Reflection by John Quinn

The lawnmowers are busy these days, but I'm beginning to wonder if mowing a lawn is really a pointless exercise. You end up with a lawn of such pristine beauty; cut with such precision that you half-expect Roger Federer to drop by and ask if he might use your lawn for much-needed practice. Pristine … for a few hours. And then it begins. A conspiracy of dandelions, popping their bright yellow, pagan heads above your sacred sward in singles, couples and ultimately arrogant clumps. Dandelions rampant, completely destroying your perfect lawn in a couple of days. Those yellow-helmeted invaders are the bane of my life. I take them on individually, laying them waste with my walking-stick, taking particular delight in savaging an entire family group, but it is ultimately a hollow victory. There is a second line waiting and, come the dawn, they will fly their flags triumphantly all across the lawn. I am genuinely considering the notion of wilderness gardening.

And then my daughter sends me a text and photo from distant Long Island. In the photo my granddaughter Riley proudly wears a floral crown made of … dandelions! 'Having fun at the Dandelion Festival,' the text explains. I need to know more. The Dandelion Festival is held annually in Southold on the north fork of Long Island, New York. It is organised by Ira, the ranch-owner who is 'big into biodynamics'. Hundreds come to his barn on Dandelion Day to hear talks on his way of living and basically how and why we should stop killing the planet we live on. There are stalls selling dandelion wine, seedlings, herbs and plants. It is very much a family day, so they have flower-crowns, potpourri-making, face-painting and chicken-petting for the children. Look kiddies, you can even have doughnuts with dandelion icing! Dandelion coffee, anyone?

So maybe it's time for second thoughts. It's time to get real and celebrate the dandelions in my life. After all, they are the first flowers to welcome the bees in early summer! And those dandelion stalks have many medicinal properties. Wonderful to add to your salads too!

I look across the carnage I have created with my walking-stick. Noble warriors struck down by an angry, ignorant giant. There are tinges of remorse. This may be the beginning of a Road to Damascus conversion. As the song says, 'All God's children got a place in the choir' – and I'm going to have to find a place for those beautiful dandelions …

God Is Always There

Mary Ann Papp

Hope sprung eternal when the 2010s passed to the 2020s here in Ireland and it continued almost until spring arrived. The storm clouds over China seemed far away and most of the Western World felt hopeful that the storm known as 'Covid-19' would either not come or be short-lived with little damage. Did the luck of the Irish, the blessings of St Patrick, cease? I think not; I hope not. For though we remain in the midst of it, the Son shines still on all who are willing and able to look upward and inward instead of down and away. I am a (New) Jersey girl living in Europe for the past eleven years. The same God who has loved and protected me – protected all of us near and far – in every storm of life continues to do so now; of that I have no doubt.

A number of years ago I travelled as a youth minister with a group of American teenagers to the National Catholic Youth Conference in Ohio. It was there I first heard the song, 'God Is Always There' by Michael Mahler. Music is the language God often uses to speak to me and this song spoke a truth I had experienced much of my life.

As a teen, I lost my father after a brief illness. That is when I first truly encountered the God of love, mercy and compassion. Until that time God was a concept I learned about in school, prayed to in my head and hoped somehow was real. But during my father's illness I saw the true, living faith of people who knew the Lord personally; people like my mom, our parish priest, my dad's doctor and neighbors. They prayed not just in the rote words of standard prayers but in sincere faith, hope and trust that, no matter the outcome, God would be there. And God was. God carried me through and lifted me up, giving me hope, perspective and a future, despite having lost my dad.

Some twenty years later, I lost my brother on 11 September 2001. His death at the World Trade

Center was sudden and traumatic. I first heard about the attack as I came out of Mass that Tuesday morning; my God, what had happened? My family gathered at my sister's home while waiting for some news of my brother's whereabouts. Instinctively we began to pray the Rosary, watching in horror as the South Tower collapsed under its own weight. 'Now and at the hour of our death.' Despite watching the moment of my brother's death on live TV, my 'Amen' was true assent, founded on the faith and confidence that, no matter the outcome, God would be there. And God was. I felt closer to the Lord in the days, weeks and months following my brother's death than probably at any other time before. God encouraged me to write and speak publicly on my experience of faith among the ashes, and I responded. Yes, the world can seem quite unfair at times, but God is always right there in the midst of it! As an adult I had embraced the ever-present God in my heart, my life and my vocation as a wife, mother and lay minster. So, when the unthinkable happened, God was already there with me. Thanks be to God!

In some ways, my experience of God during those earlier events prepared me for the sudden, stressful experience of this Covid-19 lockdown. It seems when everything we think is important fails or is taken away, we are left with what really matters, and that for me is trust and hope in our God! This year, once again, I turned to God in prayer – seeking God's comfort and consolation amidst the isolation, offering and receiving the support of others via the amazing technologies we have available, especially while I live so far away from my family.

For quite a few years I had been keeping an Instagram travel blog, where I would share some of my experiences visiting different places I had been blessed to go. Increasingly, I felt the Lord speaking to my heart about the other blessings I received: the spiritual ones I was aware of, but not sharing with others. At the start of Lent 2019, responding to the prompting of the Holy Spirit, I created an Instagram prayer journal called IrishToPray, posting the fruits of my daily prayer. It began a very intentional practice of prayer for me as each day I read the day's scripture and invited God to speak to my heart in a real and personal way. Then I would write a short reflection and post it to my page. People I know, and some I don't, like, comment and ask for prayer. I could not have anticipated when I started that more than a year ago how valuable and fruitful it would become to order my day in prayer, especially during this year's lockdown. This is the reflection I shared 20 March 2020, one year after I started IrishToPray and just one week after the Covid-19 crisis began:

'In distress you called, and I rescued you.' (Ps 81:7)

There are so many blessings to behold, so many stories of love and compassion to read and share, if only our minds and hearts are open to receive them! Just yesterday I virtually attended three communal, global prayer experiences. One of my social groups is standing virtually with a Spanish friend and her family who have all been infected with Covid-19. My bible study group will pray together today via one of the online video apps. All blessings, all gifts, all because of the pandemic.

No doubt there is pain, suffering, fear and anxiety. No doubt people are sick and dying because of it as well. But we are collectively turning towards one another despite moving physically away. And we are collectively turning toward the Lord in prayer and supplication like no other time since September 11th. And the Lord HEARS and rescues us! Will that take this pandemic away? Not likely anytime soon. But can and will our fear and anxiety, suffering and pain be lessened as we place our trust in God ...? ABSOLUTELY!!

I pray today for those with little or no faith, that they may come to know the strength, hope and love found in God through Christ Jesus our Lord. Pray with me.

Since the lockdown began in March, sometime after my morning prayer and post, I would virtually attend daily Mass via Facebook, YouTube or some other medium. Often, I 'went to Mass' in cities and towns around the world that I have either been to or would like to visit someday. Some of my favorites have been a parish in Bryanston, South Africa (where I have never been), and one in Victoria, Australia (where I have been when visiting friends). Even though the communities of faith are not present I have appreciated both the familiarity and the differences in Masses around the world! An American music minister I met at that youth conference years ago, Steve Angrisano, began praying the Chaplet of Divine Mercy in song via Facebook Live every day from his home in Texas. A few of my family and friends joined in each day and I felt a tremendous closeness to them and God. As I said, music is my God-language. If singing is praying twice, as they say, then I pray constantly! Interspersed in my day, particularly if I had trouble sleeping at night, I would turn to Our Lady by praying the Rosary;

some online versions have reflections and music that soothe my soul.

Like many people, my place of employment closed in March 2020 due to the lockdown, which left me with a lot more time at home. My husband and I had moved to a new house just before the lockdown, so we didn't have a church or neighborhood community around to support us. I felt a bit lost, to be honest, as I didn't even know the few people around me who I could physically see. During those months of aloneness, I found God in the park when I walked the dog or in the back garden when the sun shone and the spring flowers bloomed. Then, little by little, as the days warmed and the sun shone brighter and stronger, I began meeting neighbours tending their gardens or walking their dogs. Genuine care and compassion for one another grew, as we each offered help with trips to the shops, Easter candy on doorsteps and, eventually, scheduled time together outside, two meters apart. I found that God lives in my estate, in the minds, hearts and actions of the people who welcomed us to their community, generously giving of themselves to help us feel accepted and cared for.

I found God in the virtual world too! Many people have long imagined God somewhere up in the clouds, but as we embarked upon technological ministry, we learned that God actually can be spoken of, shared and received via 'the cloud!' New ways of evangelisation emerged as we moved from face-to-face to online ministry. I became involved in my new local parish by responding to a Sunday mass invitation to join a Faith Development Team they hoped to start. An email, a WhatsApp and a phone call later and I began meeting like-minded parishioners interested in learning how to meet the changing needs of our community and world, needs we cannot (at least for the time-being) meet in person. Those with the gift of technology (I think that's the eighth Gift of the Holy Spirit!) helped those less gifted learn how to use sites and apps that have since become household words! Covid could not lock down opportunities to grow in faith, to minister or to continue to feel part of the larger faith community. It took small steps of faith, often via email, to find God out there. And God was there.

One of the biggest disappointments of my lockdown experience was the inability to travel. I missed celebrating my mom's eighty-fifth birthday because I could not fly in March. Not that I missed anything really, as by then even those local to her couldn't see her in person. One of our dear friends had been sick for a few years and we missed the opportunity to see him before he passed away. Those moments we gather to celebrate and commemorate people we love were lost this year. Nothing can replace them, but our God has provided many ways to be near, even from afar.

My husband and I did, however, travel to America in late July 2020. We made the decision to fly over quickly, as it became clear that our friend was closer to the end of his life than we had known. Though we didn't want him to suffer, we did hope he would live for us to see him while we waited out the fourteen-day quarantine; instead, we received news of his passing just an hour after we landed. Matt arrived 'home' at almost the same time we did – just to different homes. The next day we went for Covid-19 tests, hoping a negative result might free us and others of concerns as we prepared for his funeral. Waiting for the results was difficult and frustrating; even expedited tests take time – time we felt we were wasting not seeing our loved ones. The outdoor funeral came and went, masks on, while my husband delivered his first-ever eulogy at the gravesite of one of his most beloved friends. The negative results arrived two days later. Was God there? Did God care about what might seem small stuff amidst a year full of global fear, suffering and frustration? Absolutely! Our socially distanced visits with family and friends boosted our spirits, our negative tests relieved some anxiety, and life felt somewhat normal again, if only briefly. God is always there; God always cares.

While I was in America, I attended Mass in a new parish, fondly (and cheekily) referred to as 'Our Lady of Zoom'! What began when a friend invited a priest to celebrate Mass with his family via 'Zoom' grew into scores of families from across the country participating in Sunday liturgy. Monsignor Robert Sheeran, retired President of Seton Hall University, a priest who was integral to all of these people's lives and faith, welcomed the opportunity to celebrate the Zoom Mass. Self-isolation wasn't easy for him, as for many priests who are used to being physically present to the faithful, especially at uncertain, difficult times. I spoke with Mgr Sheeran before returning to Ireland, and he shared his experience with me.

He was delighted when our mutual friend invited him to celebrate Mass via Zoom. Rather than broadcasting an online Mass from an empty church, this experience was interactive! The few minutes before Mass starts became the gathering space outside the sanctuary, as people shared the events of their week, simple as they were. Lectors proclaimed scripture from their own homes; virtual hugs abound as people signed off their home computer-church. Isn't this what we all crave during this pandemic: interaction, interdependence, relationship? While we may have little choice but to worship online, or in person but distant, we may as well make the best of it! For where(ever) two or more are gathered, pandemic or not, at home, online, in church, God is there; God is always there!

Monsignor Sheeran chose John Foley's 'The Cry of the Poor' as the gathering hymn at every Mass since April. The lyrics of the song acknowledge the poverty of spirit we are both called to and blessed by, and they invite us to welcome the Lord into our struggles, and brokenness. Who of us has not experienced brokenness and poverty during this lockdown? Who has not suffered in some way at the hands of this dreaded disease and global pandemic? The suffering is real: physical, financial, emotional and spiritual. The good news, the eternal good news, is that God is there. God is always there. Let us praise God in this storm, no matter how long it lasts. For the same God who has seen us through every storm continues to see us through this one. Hold fast. It may be raining now, but the Son still shines.

Spending Time with your Children

A Reflection by John Quinn

It's not easy being a parent under present circumstances – finding ways of entertaining, amusing and educating children in a situation that none of us could ever have envisaged. It's especially difficult for parents of very young children and toddlers who cannot grasp this strange new world. So, well done to the parents! You're just brilliant and you rightly deserve the title 'heroes' along with all the other carers. Take a bow!

Children are resilient, of course, and will readily respond to loving care and especially to time being spent with them. I am reminded of this by a text I got from my son Declan some years ago: 'Interesting programme on Channel 4. Check it out!' I take his advice. The programme is 'One Hundred Greatest Toys' as voted by Channel 4 viewers. As the programme unfolds, Declan is clearly reliving his childhood, texting me repeatedly as old favourites of his come up. We both wonder what will be number one on the list. We are both wrong, but Declan's wife, Kelly, guesses correctly. It is Lego – an old-fashioned toy that beats all the modern sophisticated technological gizmos out of sight.

Later, Declan sends me a final text: 'Do you remember me and you making that Lego helicopter that you got me on my seventh birthday? It was on the floor of the living room in the little house on the prairie many moons ago. It took us about two hours!' The 'little house on the prairie' was a holiday home in Rosslare. And indeed, it was 'many moons ago' – over thirty years ago, in fact. To be honest, it had become a vague memory for me, but for Declan it had been seared into his memory in frightening detail.

You can build an awful lot more than a helicopter with Lego.

For Ambo

Stephen Monaghan CM

On the 20 March 2020 I was faced with a very difficult decision. I had twenty-four hours to make up my mind to leave or stay at the mission in Ambo. Due to the Covid-19 pandemic all schools in Ethiopia were temporarily closed and the general opinion was that they would not reopen again during the academic year.

The international news was dominated by the rapid spread of Covid-19 and the disastrous consequences it imposed on so many countries in the West. As an expat living in Ethiopia, I was receiving daily emails updating me on flight cancellations to and from Addis Ababa and on 19 March I was told that the last two remaining airlines flying to Dublin were likely to pull their schedule. As such it was a simple choice: leave now or be prepared to stay for an indefinite period of time.

This ultimatum forced me to sit down and assess my situation in Ambo and I concluded that, while staying might be the choice I would make for myself, it would probably be the worst decision I could make for everyone else. In Addis Ababa some people were terrified by encountering foreigners as they were convinced they were carrying the virus. Some foreigners had even been assaulted. Indeed, friends of mine were chased out of a butcher shop by the owner.

Despite the fact that I am well known in the area where I live, Ambo is a large market town with a lot of traffic to and from the countryside. Walking around on any normal day, people, would regularly shout the word 'Ferenje' (foreigner) at me. It's always used in a friendly manner. Children are just excited to see a foreigner while adults want to gain your attention and say hello. However, since the arrival of Covid-19 some people were beginning to shout 'Covid' at me.

This was a little disconcerting of course as it had a more hostile and fearful tone to it.

It was possible in the weeks ahead that I (as the only white person in the town) could be blamed by some for spreading the sickness. Sitting quietly in prayer, I developed a strong sense that my presence in Ambo could be a real cause of worry and anxiety to country people who might be encountering me for the first time, and if hostile words were to turn into hostile actions then I would be a source of concern to the people I am living with. It seemed clear that staying in Ambo would make me more of a liability than a help. My hope was that by returning to Ireland I would be in a much better position to help local people deal with the crisis posed by Covid-19.

So, on 21 March, I decided to return home. There was a mad scramble to try and book one of the final two flights guaranteed to be leaving Addis Ababa for Ireland the next day. Despite a power cut and an inconsistent internet connection, I managed to book one of the last seats on a flight to Dublin via Dubai.

On the morning of 22 March, as I drove out the gates of the compound and headed for the airport in Addis, I had a real sense that I was abandoning all of my confrères, friends and neighbours and a true dread of the impending disaster everyone was predicting was coming their way.

We left very early so as not to draw any attention or cause a fuss. However, even at 7 a.m. there were five little boys playing together at the gate. The previous evening, I had given each of them the gift of a matchbox car which my godson had sent over with me during a previous visit home. It's impossible to describe the level of excitement and joy there was when they received such a simple toy and as we drove past them they were beaming with joy and waving the little cars at us and shouting our names.

The first confirmed case of Covid-19 in Ethiopia was announced on Friday 13 March – an ominous day at the best of times. On that day over one hundred deaf children and adults were gathered at the school in preparation for a trip to Addis Ababa early on the Saturday morning.

The school had been chosen by the 'Starkey Foundation' to benefit from their international hearing aid program. All of the students and adult deaf would have their hearing tested and, where appropriate, would be fitted with a hearing aid.

The teachers and I had spent a great deal of time preparing the students for this opportunity – helping them to understand what a hearing aid was, how it might benefit some of them and anticipating the disappointment some of them might experience if they were deemed not to be suitable candidates.

However, at 2 p.m. on Friday 13 March I got a phone call from the doctor in Addis Ababa who was organising the program. I felt a little dizzy as he broke the news that the program was cancelled. The Government were implementing an immediate ban on gatherings of over one hundred people. As I was speaking to him I was looking out into the school yard where parents and guardians were dropping off the children for the sleepover at the school and there was a great deal of excitement in the air.

The person sitting in the office with me knew something was wrong because he said my face turned a much paler shade of white than usual. We agreed not to say anything until later that that evening when all of the students had gathered and we could control what was being communicated.

I spent the rest of the afternoon downloading short videos from the WHO and UNICEF in order to try and explain what the virus was. Sharing the news about the cancellation of the visit to Addis was heart-breaking, it was obvious that the older students were devastated as they fully understood the potential associated with receiving a hearing aid.

With everyone crammed into a classroom, the last time such a gathering would be allowed, we spent over an hour helping everyone understand the reality of the virus. With the use of sign language, role play and videos – it was a very visual learning experience – everyone had a clear understanding about the danger the virus posed, how to protect themselves and how to prevent it spreading. They had also learned the new means of greeting each other with the tapping of elbows and feet.

When the session was finished the older students thanked us for the information and understood why it was not safe to travel to Addis. This display of maturity from them was a wonderful moment which helped me appreciate just how far they had progressed since first registering at the school. Most of them had come from rural districts and had no formal means of communication. (They had what we call informal sign language which is unique to their family.) As such they had no ability to properly express an emotion let alone an opinion and would not even have known their own name. So, seeing them stand up and express themselves that Friday evening was an affirmation of everything the school had set out to achieve in providing these young people with access to language and learning and self-determination.

At 2 p.m. that day when I got the fateful phone call announcing the cancellation of the program I was wondering if there was a God at all. However, at 5.30 p.m. I found myself turning to God and saying a quiet prayer of gratitude and thanksgiving. We had managed to come a very long way without hearing aids and that journey would continue regardless.

Over the weekend it was announced that all schools in Ethiopia would close for two weeks from Tuesday 17 March. However, given what was happening elsewhere in the world, we had a strong inclination that the school would probably not open again for this academic year.

Before I departed Ambo, one little girl named Chaltu, aged seven, was in the school office with her dad. She is our youngest student and incredibly bright and determined to learn. I asked her to sign the alphabet and she got as far as 'Q' before getting a little mixed up, so we completed it together. I was saddened to think about the disruption the virus was going to cause for her education as she was making such good progress.

Many parents of the children at the school tell us about the very negative attitude people in the rural areas have regarding children who are deaf or born with a disability. Many consider a deaf child as incapable of learning and a burden on the family. As such these children are often hidden away and live very lonely and isolated lives.

I think I can say for certain that after six months at the Ambo Lazarist Deaf School there is no way Chaltu could ever be hidden away. In that short time, she had developed a wonderful spirit and was more than capable of holding her own with the older students. Also, her father had become very engaged in her learning and was enrolled in our sign language course. Unfortunately, this initiative also fell victim to Covid-19.

Bole Airport, Addis Ababa, is one of the fastest growing airports in the world. Normally it takes well over an hour to get through all the various security checks. On the 22 March, it resembled a ghost town and took less than fifteen minutes to get from the carpark to the departures lounge. Inside the terminal I got my first real glimpse of the doomsday scenario that was playing out on the media and it was very disconcerting. Most people were in transit and so were wearing masks (such items were not yet available in Ethiopia). Some people were completely decked out with full PPE: masks, suits, goggles and gloves. I felt as if I was in a laboratory rather than an airport. Without a mask I felt a little vulnerable and became obsessive about using antibacterial gel each and every time I touched anything, be it a trolly, a bag or a door.

Arriving into Dublin we were greeted by people handing out leaflets encouraging us to self-isolate or restrict our movements for fourteen days. The first bit of news I received when I exited the airport related to the death of a man I knew well who was one of the very first victims of Covid-19 in Ireland. Suddenly the awful reality of the virus and its consequences became very real.

Later that morning I participated in a podcast which was exploring how other countries around the world were fairing with the pandemic. Given how things were playing out here in Ireland, I had a deep sense of dread and foreboding for the people I had left behind in Ambo. I had visited the two hospitals in the town and knew that they were ill equipped to deal with the potential crisis that lay ahead. However, being home meant I now had the opportunity to try and do something to help in some way.

The information coming from Ethiopia indicated that the virus was spreading at a slower rate throughout the country than it was in Europe and the death rate was also relatively lower. There were various theories as to why this was happening, such as the fact that developing countries have experience in dealing with large outbreaks of disease and thus have mechanisms in place that allow them to respond more rapidly. Whatever the reason, the virus itself was not the most immediate threat to people, rather it was the economic fallout from the lockdown that had been imposed by the government and the fact that nearly all trade, locally, nationally and internationally had ceased.

In Ambo, the majority of people I know are day labourers. This effectively means they live hand to mouth. Their average daily wage is about €2.00. Most people do not have access to banks or savings. They buy their daily food from the small roadside markets. The staple diet is 'Injera' (a traditional pancake type food) and some 'Wot' a sauce made of chickpea flour and spices. Potatoes, pasta and rice are also part of the staples as they can be stored for a period of time. However, with no income, the markets shut and people being ordered to stay at home, families were struggling to put food on the table for their children.

Living in lockdown in Ireland seemed to be putting limitations not only on physical movements but on my mental ability to adjust to being stuck in one place and not having direct contact with other people. Returning to Ireland increased my own sense of expectation or obligation about doing something to assist the people I had left behind. Yet, I found myself sitting around each day, adhering to government guidelines, limiting my movements and contacts and feeling a little hopeless that there was anything I could do to assist. However, St Vincent de Paul was a great believer in divine providence.

He understood that there will be periods of time when very little will happen in our lives and we will wonder what is the purpose, but if we are patient and trusting, then the time for action will present itself. You just need to be tuned into the Spirit. And, he says, when that time comes you need to be decisive in your response. I was receiving many messages describing the difficult situation of people in Ambo and so it was rather difficult to trust this maxim.

I shared what I knew with various people including the Ethiopia Deaf Project (Ireland), a small but dedicated group of people who are committed to raising funds to support the deaf school. They responded by putting out an urgent appeal on Facebook. There was a generous response. It resulted in enough money being raised to help provide food parcels for seventy-five families.

Thanks to the good will and desire of some people to help, a couple of online fundraising events were proposed. The Ethiopia Deaf Project decided to move their annual sponsored cycle of

West Cork online and the parents' association in St Vincent's Castleknock College suggested organising an online event to engage the students to take part in a charitable activity during lockdown. When we were planning these events, the one big challenge was how best to promote these events and encourage as many people as possible to participate.

Given St Vincent's absolute trust in providence, he might not be surprised by what took place, but I certainly could not believe it when, apropos of something else, I received a phone call from a journalist in RTÉ, Mr Aengus Cox. This led to an invite for to do a short interview on *Morning Ireland* about my work in Ethiopia. Of course, it also provided the perfect platform to promote the two fundraising initiatives.

The response to the interview was very positive and I received some very encouraging messages from people all over Ireland. It confirmed the power of the national media to help get a message out to people. But the real work involved marrying the publicity the interview provided with the additional capability that social media offers to engage with a whole other group of people. The fact that the interview was transcribed and featured on RTÉ News Now enabled many of my friends in Irish deaf community to engage with the story and also get involved. It was, as St Vincent would say, time now to act decisively.

The four days following the interview saw my phone 'screen time' increase by about five hundred per cent as I spent all day and sometimes much of the night engaging with people on social media, sharing the story, responding to messages, guiding people to our donations page, thanking others and so on. Despite all of the trials and problems that Irish people were experiencing during the lockdown, there was still a tremendous capacity in people to see beyond their own circumstances and respond to people in a worse situations.

Most of the people I know in Ambo enter each new day with no guarantee of work, income or food. They head out into the world and all they have is a sense that God will provide, and some days God does not provide much. After the first month of the pandemic I was wondering what opportunity God might provide for me to responded to the needs of people. By the time we had finished our online fundraising events, we had managed to:

- Provide over six hundred food parcels to around 250 families.
- Pay the salaries of the teachers at the kindergarten school. (The loss of student fees meant there was no income to pay salaries and we were in danger of losing some of our staff who are all qualified in Montessori teaching.)
- Complete the building of a new classroom which the local government insisted was necessary to guarantee social distancing and ensure the school could open for the new academic year.
- Build a new sanitising water station at the deaf school to ensure the children could practise proper hand hygiene when they returned to school.

The following quote from St Vincent de Paul captures how I felt at the end of all of this:

Do not limit your vision any longer to yourself, but see the Lord around you and in you, ready to put his hand to the work as soon as you ask for his help. You will see that all will go well.[1]

The people in the village where the deaf school is located have a real affection for Ireland. Each year for the past ten years groups of boys from two Vincentian schools have travelled to Ambo to help run a summer school for the local children. Up to 250 children can turn up each day. During that time the boys immerse themselves in the culture and life of the people, with visits to the markets to purchase local crafts, invitations to the social housing project – they may even be invited to a wedding or find themselves in attendance at a funeral, both of which are quite unique experiences.

They also visit the Leprosy Project, which was established by the Vincentian Fathers some thirty years ago. The houses provided people suffering from the illness with stability and the opportunity to receive treatment for their illness. It takes six months to a year to properly treat leprosy, at which point the person is cured and are no longer contagious. However, they will always have to live with the disfiguring effects of the disease. Thankfully, there has been no new case of leprosy in Ambo for over twenty years.

The visit to this particular project is often fraught with anxiety for the boys. When one group arrived at the project and encountered a couple of women who had been affected by leprosy, they froze and went into a little huddle. I was beginning to think they might not enter the community centre. However, some children from the summer school who live in the village came and took them by the hands and led them inside.

The boys received a warm welcome from the Chairperson and were given a comprehensive overview of leprosy: from identification, to prevention, to treatment.

When they were leaving the project each of the boys spontaneously embraced the women who only an hour earlier seemed to be the cause of so much anxiety. This embrace meant a lot to the women as well, as they are still very much stigmatised and marginalised by their appearance. It was a real example of how education and an opportunity to meet and engage with people who we perceive as something of a threat can help to break down fear and prejudice.

Unfortunately, this year, due to the Covid-19 pandemic, all of the excitement and the energy that the Irish boys bring to Ambo was missing, but the local people said 'even though they are not among us, we know they are still with us. Their kindness and generosity have helped us through a very difficult time. The only thing we have to offer in return is to ask God's blessing on everyone who had helped.'

The local conference of St Vincent de Paul was asked to coordinate the distribution of the food parcels. So great was the demand that the conference invited new members to join, and together they managed to distribute over 650 food parcels to around 250 families. It is hoped that the expansion of the St Vincent de Paul society will allow for even more engagement in the lives of poor people struggling with various problems. As St Vincent de Paul said: 'We should assist the poor in every way and do it both by ourselves and by enlisting the help of others…. To do this is to preach the gospel by words and work.'[2]

So where was God in all of this? I believe God was present:

- At the heart of my decision to come back to Ireland. Sometimes it's only in the silence of prayer that things become clear and you can make the right decision (even if the decision is opposed to what you might desire for yourself).
- In the generosity and kindness of people who responded to plight of people in Ambo.
- In the solidarity that the parents and boys of St Vincent's college showed for the people who have taken great care of the boys over the years.

- In the willingness of the parishioners here in St Justin's Parish in Ambo (many of whom were themselves struggling) to volunteer and join the Society of St Vincent de Paul to assist with the outreach to families, especially in the leprosy and social housing projects. Hopefully the Society will now go from strength to strength.
- In the opportunity to have the time and space required develop a website for the school (www.alds.info) that helps tell its story.

And where was God for the people in Ambo? There was a real sense among the people there that God had listened to their prayer and responded to their need. They in turn asked God to bless all those who generously supported them. I have been privileged to receive such a blessing several times and its quite a powerful thing. I remember in particular one old woman who came to the church to say thanks for some financial assistance she received to allow her to attend the hospital. She stood in front of me and spontaneously composed her own little 'psalm', an open and heartfelt prayer begging God to grant me health and happiness, peace in my heart, protection for family and all the strength I need to continue my work. I remember closing my eyes and I could really feel the power of her intentions wash over me. There were many such blessings showered down on all those who helped in some way to ease the difficulties of people in Ambo.

The cancellation of the hearing aid was of course a let-down for the students, but the fact that all of the deaf community were gathered at the school on 13 March was also something of a blessing. It meant we were able to provide accurate information about the virus, reducing some of the anxiety and fear that would have resulted if the students were getting such knowledge second hand. We were the first school in Ambo to get the news about the virus, the first to begin educating the students about how to protect and prevent the spread of the virus and also the first to begin modelling a new way of greeting each other socially.

Presently we are waiting for the Government to announce the official date for the opening of schools. Already some new students have turned up to register. We hope God will continue to bless our efforts to support these children to receive an education through generous support of people. All we can do is follow the advice of St Vincent: 'We must put our cares and concerns into his hands, for he will never fail.'[3]

ENDNOTES

1   Correspondence to Louis Rivet, 19 December 1655, in M. Poole
    (ed.), *Vincent De Paul: Correspondence, Conferences, Documents*,
    Vol. 5, New York: New City Press, 1995, p. 494.

2   Vincent De Paul, Conference to the Congregation of the Mission,
    6 December 1658, in Pierre Coste CM (Ed. and Trans.) *St Vincent
    De Paul: Correspondence, Conferences, Documents*, Vol. 12, New
    York: New City Press, 1995, p. 66.

3   Louis Abelly, *The Life of the Venerable Servant of God*, Vol. 3, New
    York: New City Press, 1993, p. 24. https://via.library.depaul.
    edu/abelly_english/4; accessed on 1 January 2021.

Fear

A Reflection by John Quinn

In our present circumstances, fear can play a dominant role in our lives – fear of illness, fear of the unknown, fear of the future. The late John O'Donohue often spoke about fear. He told a classic story of fear from India.

A man is condemned to spend a night in a cell with a poisonous snake. If he moves, the snake will attack and kill him. So he spends the night standing in a corner, frozen with fear, eyeing the coiled deadly threat in the opposite corner. The night wears on. The man desperately fights off sleep and is relieved to welcome the dawn. The snake never moves. When the full light of day comes into the cell, the 'snake' is revealed as an innocuous coil of rope.

Fear insinuates itself so much into our lives – fear of the unknown, of failure, of being ourselves, of illness, of death. And yet, so often it turns out to be a pile of old rope that petrifies us; groundless fears that immobilise us. We waste the night waiting for the dawn.

What we have to do, John says, is to face up to our fear and name it. When we do that, the fear will begin to shrink. 'What am I afraid of?' is a very liberating question, John suggests. Easier said than done, of course, but he reminds us that there is lots of encouragement in the Bible. According to John, the phrase 'Be not afraid' occurs 366 times in the Good Book – 'One for every day in the year', John laughs, 'and one for luck!'

In the Midst

Clare Gilmore

INTRODUCTION

As 2019 came to an end I was working in Drumalis Retreat Centre in Larne, Co. Antrim, and we were planning ahead for the next season of parish retreats. For many dioceses, 2020 lent itself to a play on words regarding our ability to see and having 'perfect vision' to see God at work in our lives. In Drumalis, we had decided to dedicate 2020 as a year of focus on 'The God Who Speaks'.

Roll on a few months and the world has a new vocabulary. As the lives of millions of people became affected, words and phrases like 'lockdown', 'pandemic', 'coronavirus', 'Covid-19', 'key workers', 'Zoom', 'self-isolate', 'social distancing', 'Covidiot', 'elbow-bump', 'furlough' and 'bubble' all took on a new familiarity. As each of our lives changed, almost overnight, the words we spoke and the gestures we made became heightened and more serious.

It is into this scene that I look back, that I reflect on the months that have passed from March until now, and that I try to place where it is I have heard God's voice, and what it is I have heard God say to me.

NAMING ALOUD

One of the saving graces I've had during the pandemic is that my monthly spiritual direction didn't stop. Instead, my director offered to meet with me via Skype and, while I had an initial hesitation to this (unsure that a virtual meeting would hold the same sense of openness and sharing that our face-to-face meetings had), I soon learned that God can communicate through all manner of things – and my laptop was one of them! In meeting with my spiritual director, I was able to name aloud the experiences I was having as the pandemic unfolded and reflect on where God was in the middle of it all. The answers didn't always come easily, and, to be honest, most of the time I simply had to sit with the questions, hoping that at some point things would begin to fit together. I would like to share some of these experiences with you now, offering something of what they mean to me a few months on.

ONE: I LIVE ALONE

There's a saying: 'Be careful what you wish for, you might just get it.'

Like many people, I find that life can be busy – sometimes very busy! I live in a lovely rented apartment by myself, and between working, volunteering and visiting friends and family, I sometimes felt that all I did was sleep in my apartment rather than actually live there. There were evenings as I was driving home that I wished I had more free time to just hang out at home, read books, listen to music and have more time to enjoy my own company. I was wistful for all the things I would do – if only I had time.

2020. Just a few months in and my wish came true. The country went into 'lockdown' and no-one was allowed to leave their home except for essential travel. Having gone self-employed to work in church ministry, I now found that churches were closed and I had no work to go to.

There are a couple of things that strike me about this time. First is the overwhelming loneliness and isolation that swept over my soul. I felt it in every moment of the day. When I woke up, the first thing I heard was silence. Before, I used to cherish that silence; it held a depth of stillness and tranquillity that I would allow to wash over me and sink into my inner being, preparing me for the day ahead. But now all I could feel was the dead weight of nothingness that it held. As morning passed, I would move from room to room again just to break up the day. On the days that I felt up to it, I would sit at the computer and write; on the days that I didn't, I would just sit on the sofa, seemingly immobile. All the while the silence grew. Sure, I turned on the TV and I listened to the radio, but none of these things filled the growing emptiness. In fact, they even seemed to add to my sense of separation, as did phone calls with my parents and Zoom calls with my boyfriend. Evening would fall, another day would be done and another layer was added to my sadness.

I was alone and I felt alone. Yet I am a person of faith, and I believe that we are never alone. Jesus' very last words to his disciples when he ascended into heaven were to remind us that we would never be alone. He said: 'Remember, I am with you always, to the end of the age' (Mt 28:20). I knew this, and I sensed this. In my sessions with my spiritual director I would acknowledge that while I felt incredibly alone, I knew that there was someone else in the apartment with me. While I didn't feel God's presence in a physical way, I felt it instinctually. It was like the smell of perfume or aftershave that lingers even when the person who wore it isn't there. In the silence that threatened to deafen, I heard the voice of God tell me I was not alone. I saw the face of God Who Accompanies Me in the midst of everything.

The other thing that hits me is how things fell into place when everything else seemed to fall apart. Let me explain. There's a joke that goes: 'How do you make God laugh?' The answer: 'Tell him your plans!' Well, like many of you reading this, I had 2020 all planned out. For me, it was the year I got the courage to leave the security of full-time employment and work for myself (or as I saw it, God). I would spend spring and autumn going to parishes every other week working alongside the Redemptorists on missions and novenas; and during the summer, I would get a job temping. It sounded good to me, until twelve weeks later when the plan fell apart.

I may as well confess now that 'trust' comes up regularly for me in spiritual direction, along with the fact that I like to cover my bases and have a plan B 'just in case'. What I find myself wondering, though, is what does this say about my trust – or lack thereof – in God's promise to provide? My experience in the pandemic has, yet again, shown to me the God Who Keeps Promises. Within weeks of having no work, I began to get regular shifts as an agency care worker. I started visiting people's homes at a time when everyone else was banned from doing so and this became a fount of great grace for me. Not only did I encounter wonderful people, I got to hear God speak to me through them. In the midst of my own isolation and loneliness, I met men and women for whom lockdown was part of their norm, yet they were so full of life and vibrancy. We chatted, and over the months that followed I learned the importance of gratitude; of noticing the small gifts each day brings and being thankful for them all. I experienced that God Who Keeps Promises is also God Who Provides; providing not just for my material well-being, but for my spiritual well-being also. God is indeed good.

TWO: I'M ALL OVER THE PLACE

Living in Ireland, I'm well accustomed to changeable weather and the adage of having 'four seasons in one day'. While I consider myself a balanced and emotionally stable person, I would forgive you for questioning this had you seen me when the pandemic hit! Not being someone who easily cries, it came as a complete shock to find myself sitting on the couch (too many days to count), caught between deep shudders of inconsolable sobbing and bouts of stunned silence. To be honest, even admitting here that this is what I did is difficult for me. But it is the truth, and there is always something to be learned from the truth.

I'm still not sure I can completely put to words what I experienced in the first few months of the pandemic, but a passage from the Book of Job stands out. Job is in a sorry state, and when three of his friends hear of his troubles they come to visit him, wishing to console and comfort him. However, when they see him we are told that 'they sat with him on the ground seven days and seven nights, and no one spoke a word to him, for they saw that his suffering was very great' (Job 2:11–13). There's something about this that resonates with me – something about being silenced by the immensity of a moment; being caught by whatever it is the moment brings and finding it temporarily take possession of you. The only thing I found I could do was to submit – to sit, day or night, and experience in that moment whatever emotion it was that presented itself to me.

I have a deep sense that God was sending these moments of overwhelming emotion to ready me for the world we all now find ourselves living in – this world of uncertainty and sudden newness. In this experience I have met God of the Present Moment. Whether I have felt overwhelmed by fear (for my parents, for the future, for loved ones), by grief (for all that we have lost), or by bewilderment (not knowing what to do or think or feel); or whether I have felt blanketed by a sense of 'all will be well', of calm, of hope, of reassurance, of strength – the overriding experience I had is of God Who Soothes Me and whispers 'Shh'.

It seems to me we are all simply feeling our way into the future. None of us know what the future holds. We never have. However, perhaps we each feel it more intensely now. What we do know is who holds the future; and we walk into that future knowing that God walks alongside us, and whispers 'Shh. Be still. Be still and know that I am God' (cf. Ps 46:10).

THREE: WHAT ABOUT TOUCH?

There's nothing more natural in the world than touch; than reaching out and physically connecting with another. I remember listening to a Radio 4 programme and an older woman rang in to share that the reason she went to a weekly dance class and loved it so much is that it was the only time in the whole week that she was touched! Imagine! The sad thing is that even before Covid, there were hundreds who could identify with this woman. They could go months and not experience the touch of another human. What if, as a result of Covid, by losing touch, we lose each other? This is the question I have been asking myself and asking God.

As an auntie to seven nieces and nephews (aged between four and twelve) I can't stop myself asking what kind of world are they going to grow up in? I hear them say 'don't forget to keep your distance' and that's the very place my fear hinges – what if they *don't* forget? What if our young people grow up in a world without touch? A world where everyone is suspicious of everyone else? A world where a core part of what makes us human, truly human (and humane) is no longer nurtured?

When I questioned God about our losing touch, he responded with his own touch. As I tuned in to online Masses, I found myself comforted and reassured by gospel passages telling of Jesus reaching out and touching others in the midst of their exclusion. Social distancing is not a new concept; even in Jesus' time there were social constraints around touch and illness, with a great many people literally labelled 'untouchable'. Instructions were issued to keep your distance from these people, and from others (such as tax collectors and sinners). However, God is God Who Touches. It is central to who God is, and it is central to who we are.

CONCLUSION

In the midst of all that has unfolded in 2020, God has not been hidden. My spiritual direction has enabled me to see where he has been speaking to me and revealing who God is. I have met God Who Accompanies Me; God Who Keeps Promises; God Who Provides; God of the Present Moment; God Who Soothes Me; and God Who Touches, and for that I am forever grateful and will forever praise Gods goodness. Amen.

Alone

A Reflection by John Quinn

You don't have to be a Liverpool fan to sing 'You'll Never Walk Alone' (I'm a Chelsea fan and believe me that involves a lot of walking alone!). Ok, they've won the League title, but the anthem was only borrowed from the musical 'Carousel'.

When I do my twenty-lap walk around my garden – alone – I am distracted by a symphony of birdsong soaring above me, the music coming from an orchestra of the tiniest throats, all rejoicing in spring. Before me, the cherry tree is about to explode into bud and will soon be a riot in pink. Over the hedge comes the sound of sliotar on camán as the neighbour's children hone their skills. A promise of brighter days when the big boys and girls come out to play again. Johnny from across the road breezes in on his ride-on mower, cuts my grass and is gone in ten minutes with a cheery wave.

My neighbours Maureen and Fergus phone me regularly to know if I need shopping done. Their son Colin delivers the shopping every Wednesday. Their daughter Celine drops in the *Irish Times* daily, regular as clockwork. Rosemary has delivered a loaf of her delicious brown bread while Mary from down the road left a bag of gorgeous scones on my windowsill. Every Sunday Joe delivers a beautiful hot lunch. And as for Lisa's lasagne and Kelly's and Celine's 'spag bol' … the list goes on and on. My children phone almost daily and send cheery videos – grandson learning to ride a bike, granddaughter draws a family tree to include all her stuffed toys …

I have just had the most wonderful holiday in France without ever leaving my armchair reading Peter Mayle's *A Year in Provence* (thanks Pauline!). David Attenborough has been my personal guide to the grandeur of God in the most exotic locations. My CD collection and various radio channels (especially Lyric FM) offer me the continuing balm of the music I love. I join the community in praying the Mass on radio with my local priest Fr Barry. I am connected and far from alone. I leaf through a photo album (remember those?) recalling the most pleasant occasions with my beautiful wife and our three marvellous children. As Brendan Kennelly wrote, 'Memory gives us roses in December'. Now comes the postman with warm letters and cards from distant friends.

I make an occasional foray to the Post Office to be welcomed with a smile by Noreen and James. And James has the best-stocked general store this side of Ike Godsey's store on Walton's Mountain. On the way home I nip into the house of God for a quiet moment with the best company of all…

Alone? I have never been more un-alone in my entire life!

Standing in Solidarity

Peter Birkinshaw

I suppose it could seem quite bizarre and distant if I were to begin with the story of creation as accounted for in the Book of Genesis to assess the whereabouts of God during the Covid-19 lockdown. However, during this traumatic period of uncertainty it is in fact through our created nature that I have witnessed God at work within the individual and society as a whole. As a practising Catholic, married with the blessing of two beautiful children, the anxiety of balancing work life, study and family life during lockdown all cohered to create an unwanted level of stress and unbalance. The situation I found myself in was that similar to thousands of other families throughout Ireland, all worried about the security of work, exam results and, most importantly, the health and wellbeing of family members. On returning from work one evening I became drawn to enter a neighbouring village church to have a quiet moment of prayer and reflection. I had all the worries and anxieties mentioned and a deep sense of helplessness and lack of control over what may or may not happen in my life.

Of course I still had those anxieties and worries when leaving the church. There was no miracle moment of overwhelming calm or serenity. On the contrary, all seemed much the same. In a way, the Covid-19 pandemic could be used as a strong-arm argument by any atheist as to the lack of a loving God, although this view perhaps echoes the mockery of Christ by the chief priests and elders during the crucifixion of our Lord (Mt 27:39-44). What did happen however was that over the following few days I began to view this pandemic and the reaction to it by people very differently. The manifestation of being made in the image and likeness of our creator (Gn 1:27) was becoming tangible. Through the people

I encountered, I began to see the action of an immanent God. We find in the Book of Genesis that God breathed life into humankind (Gn 2:7); we became animated with a soul which consists of a mind with which to know and a heart with which to love. It seemed to me that only when we are stripped of our comforts and are situated in the eye of a storm does our love for others and our ability to reason overarch any wealth or material good that we previously idolised. This hit home for me one afternoon when one of my daughters began to cry because she missed her friends and had not seen them for several weeks. This was no mere whimper of boredom, behind her tears lay a deep sense of loss, a longing to be reunited; part of her childhood was missing and her dad could not replace it with anything. No amount of snakes and ladders, Uno, Netflix or tablet time was going to fix this; we are obviously made for a far higher fulfilment.

Olive, an elderly member of our local church, called by my house to drop off the parish newsletter one evening and told me that she had just finished broadcasting the Holy Rosary over the parish radio. She explained that over the past few weeks she had never prayed so much for people around the world who were affected by the Covid-19 pandemic. All people, nations and cultures; the poor, sick and grieving; people she had never even met were incorporated onto her prayers. To Olive, these people were not considered strangers, alien or foreign, but neighbours – fellow human beings who are important to her and loved by her. Olive was completely unaware that she oozed grace; she is the epitome of a disciple of Christ, who through her words and deeds has become a window to our Lord. Olive told me that she had to go and lie down because she was exhausted. This tired elderly lady made me come to realise that we do not have to act on the global stage or political podium to become effective members of society or even the Church. During the Covid-19 storm her focus on Christ did not waver; her mind's eye was clearly fixed on Jesus. She was not afraid or anxious, but devoted and steadfast. The image and likeness of God became manifest through Olive's words and deeds; her soul was and still is correctly ordered towards its creator. This paradigm transcends the realm of things that do not last in order to become united in the truth of the divine, and it is that truth that we all long for. This all may sound a little surreal. Words like transcendence, truth and unity can come across as being a bit 'new age' and fluffy, but if we examine how we have ordered ourselves during this deadly viral outbreak one can view how we have ordered ourselves back to God, in unity, in solidarity and in love, as gracefully displayed by Olive.

This solidarity was never more palpable than during a funeral procession that I witnessed several weeks into lockdown. I knew that Church guidelines lay on the side of precaution and were limiting attendees during a funeral Mass by allowing only a small number of immediate family members, but when passing through a nearby village I was deeply moved to see a united community, standing in solidarity. With the correct distance required between each person, they lined the main road to the church. This uniform vision of fellowship continued for over a mile in length. This was a united community that understood that although the Covid-19 virus may have restricted mass gatherings and bound them to conformity, the human person will instinctively search for a reorientation in order to find ways of becoming united with the loved ones who have lost a beloved family member. During this tragic period our natural capacity to love and be in relationship with others far outweighs any obstacle that may try to extinguish our innate goodness and recognition of Gods transcendent love and providence. One can evidently see the proof of the innate goodness that lies within us due to the sheer number of volunteers who signed up to respond to the rallying call from the HSE, who were in need of support staff to assist in the public health sector. Within days of the call, the department received over five times as many former health care workers as necessary; a sure sign of self sacrifice and love of neighbour.

During lockdown we have used our knowledge and reason to attain what our hearts really desire. The technology we used in order to scroll through endless images and videos of the latest consumer goods, memes and dance routines are now being used to see the faces of our loved ones, bridging the gap between the young and the vulnerable. The ferocious unstoppable appetite that is consumerism seems to be shelved in favour of seeing the soft peachy face of our nan or grandad, or our siblings who are across the other side of the world, also in lockdown. Our innate nature strives for relationship – we yearn for communion with others. Clearly it is not good for humankind to be alone, isolated and separated from the ones we love (cf. Gn 2:18).

So if I'm asked where God was during lockdown, then I can honestly answer that he has been manifest through the hearts and minds of his creation, the creation that he deemed 'very good' (Gn 1:31). All those who have self-sacrificed in the search for responsible fellowship, truth, love, goodness and solidarity all mirror the immanent creator whether they realise this or not. Through the eyes of faith it all seems quite clear. Though some people may say that this is just a subjective vision viewed through rose-tinted glasses, I would disagree, as it is very hard to argue against the fact that during this very difficult, traumatic period our moral compass has sought to align itself back towards the things that really matter; that is, our love for one another, our own selves, our environment and God. Failure to recognise the image and likeness of God within us renders our hearts and minds to a continual spiral of unease, a helter-skelter in which the soul relentlessly searches for a possible worldly wisdom that will grant it rest. We become embroiled in whatever standards we create and in doing so we empty the cross of its power, which is the failure to recognise the wisdom of God. This creates a division within each and every one of us, starving the soul of the 'solid food' (Heb 5:14) and relationships for which it was created.

On a local level I have been witness to men and women who seek what is good, who do lift their gaze to the truth that transcends them and who, through the grace of God, realise the image and likeness of God in their neighbour. Therefore, during lockdown I heard God through the parish radio. He was in front of me when I received the newsletter. He was to the left and right sides of those who lined the road to the local church. He was behind the smiling eyes of our loved ones who appear on our screens. And he was in the heart and mind of the one who wiped away the tears from the eyes of his children.

A Salute to James

A Reflection by John Quinn

During the pandemic crisis, our local stores have served us well. We thank them most sincerely. If I may single one out, I would like to pay tribute to the one and only James Kelly.

> For pencils and pads, markers and jotters,
> All to help the home-schooling swotters.
> For spices and pasta, peas, beans and
> noodles,
> And, of course, toilet rolls, of which you
> had oodles.
> For medications and creams, for pills and
> for potions,
> And liquid refreshments, of which you had
> oceans.

For Noreen in her office – she deserves a
  mention –
Handling all that mail and payments and
  pensions.
For bread and for cakes, biscuits and treats,
For crisps and for chocolates and all kinds
  of sweets.
For *Old Moore's Almanac*, papers and mags,
And – God forgive us all – for cigars and
  for fags.
For cleaners, detergents, washing powders
  galore,
Not to mention all that hardware down the
  back of the store.
For eggs and milk and bacon and cheeses,
And a freezer chock-full of food that did
  please us.
For batteries and bulbs and chargers and
  leads,
For all our possible emergency needs.
For carrots and turnips and Kinvara
  potatoes,

For oranges and lemons, apples and
'tomaytoes'.
For flour and for cereals, for jams and for
honey,
And on every shelf always value for money.
For sardines and meatballs, soups – powder
or tinned –
And for smoked salmon – oh Lord, I have
sinned!
For coal and for gas, for logs and briquettes,
Seed for the birds and food for the pets.
For hats, gloves and towels, and thick
woollen socks,
For brollies and mops, kettles and alarm
clocks.
For all these and more – the list is unending
– Where else would we rather be
spending?
We thank you, James. With courtesy and
care
You served us so well. You were always
there.

God Willing

Andrew Watson

At the start of 2020 my wife and I had a number of things we were happily anticipating. In addition to new ministry possibilities, we looked forward to a probable graduation ceremony for our youngest daughter in Warwick with a celebratory trip to a Shakespeare production in Stratford-upon-Avon. We had also booked a holiday on the continent for just the two of us. Of course, all had to be cancelled or postponed when the Covid-19 pandemic forced everyone into varying degrees of 'lockdown'. None of us have had quite the year we expected!

Our hearts go out to those families who have suffered tragedy and loss. It has been agonising for those unable to visit loved ones in hospital or even gather for a proper funeral wake. I have an abiding image from Easter weekend of standing by an open grave, fulfilling a prior request of the deceased by playing Jim Reeves singing 'This world is not my home' from my iPod for a tiny number of spread out mourners.

Bereavement, redundancy, isolation and deep anxiety over all the uncertainty are undoubtedly taking a toll this year. And yet, ironically, the crisis has also created new opportunities for human resourcefulness. It has even prompted some to reflect more deeply on what really matters in life and rediscover faith.

At first it was a novelty, families spending more time together at home. Children were delighted as Mammy and Daddy took them walking and cycling and unearthed board games to play. April and May had weeks of unusually dry, sunny weather. In our estate, gardens were immaculate, cars gleamed and the local Tesco (one of the few places staying open) quickly sold out of fence paint!

We were happy to stand outside each week and applaud healthcare and other frontline workers. We were 'in this together'. The rise of public-mindedness felt good. OK, the shop was out of pasta and toilet roll but we hadn't lost our sense of humour and the crowds volunteering to help in any way possible were so encouraging. Some of us prayed that, while none of us like to see trouble and difficulty, this crisis might be the catalyst towards a more appreciative and less selfish world.

As a parish minister, something that has frankly been frustrating is how the risk of infection has hindered me visiting some of the very people most longing for company and the comfort of someone to pray with them. One elderly lady was counting the Sundays since she last attended worship. Another gentleman, tears in his eyes, wondered when, if ever, he'd be back.

We have all had to improvise. I've spoken and prayed with people in their yards and gardens or over the phone. There have been meetings with a dozen people dotted around a hall that normally seats a hundred. One thing that has become something of a phenomenon is how churches have taken to the internet. Clergy have posted video recordings or used live social media to bring readings and prayers to a wider than usual audience online. One Sunday we featured video greetings from members and friends all over Ireland, not to mention Australia, Portugal, Jamaica and Florida!

Personally, I've enjoyed the creative challenge of uploading weekly Bible readings, usually aided and abetted by my wife on camera duties. Mostly we've filmed me just sitting at home or standing in the empty church building, but occasionally we've gone for more 'exotic' locations like the garden shed, a local restaurant, Fanad Lighthouse or the salon of my wonderfully co-operative hairdresser! The consistent element, whatever the setting, has been the truth being introduced and read from the Bible.

Our church buildings in North Donegal had to close the weekend after St Patrick's Day and could only reopen in late July with strict social distancing measures in place. Two out of every three pews were cordoned off. No hugs or handshakes. No congregational hymns at first. (That was tough as Presbyterians like to sing!) No after-service tea and coffee and traybakes. (And believe me, we have some of the finest home-bakers in Ireland!)

Still, it was good to open the doors and welcome folk into God's house and hear voices being lifted in prayer together again. Good also, to read God's word and seek comfort and wisdom. Where was our Heavenly Father in all this? Here we were in the 'Valley of Shadow', would the Good Shepherd stay with us and bring us through?

Quite early on in lockdown I was sharing some thoughts on prayer inspired by a passage in Matthew 6. It is part of Jesus' famous 'Sermon on the Mount' where he says that in contrast to some who perform eloquent prayers to receive adulation from a human audience, believers shouldn't be afraid to 'go into your room, close the door and pray to your Father' more modestly and sincerely, yet with the confidence God knows and cares about our needs.

For the first time, I realised that the Lord is here echoing a lesser known passage from an Old Testament prophet which seemed to have an uncanny relevance for the Covid-19 crisis. Seven hundred years previously Isaiah had said, 'Go my people into your rooms and shut the doors behind you; hide yourselves for a little while until [God's] wrath has passed by' (Is 26).

On the one hand, this chapter of Isaiah contains solemn warning for those who stubbornly disregard God and his commands. Such attitudes and behaviour invite judgement! Global crises should make us think seriously of the numerous apocalyptic passages in the Bible which soberly predict a future day when the whole of mankind shall stand before our maker and have to give account for the choices we've made.

But on the other hand, this same passage contains tender assurances of grace for those who turn from doing wrong and trust in God. He will bring about new life and security. The trouble will pass. God's faithful people are promised an inheritance in 'the new Jerusalem'. Therefore, even in our present trials we can gratefully pray using Isaiah's words, 'You will keep in perfect peace those whose minds are steadfast, because they trust in you.'

If folk are considering their lifestyle more humbly in the light of scripture and praying more sincerely than before then something worthwhile has indeed come out of lockdown!

It was a dull, wet morning in July as restrictions were beginning to ease that saw our house buzzing with celebration. Our youngest daughter had just received her results and, having completed her exams online, had been awarded a First Class Honours degree in history and German. The day before had dawned a beautiful bright morning in County Down. Our outdoor pursuits instructor son, his girlfriend and I enjoyed some mountain biking around forest trails near the picturesque shores of Strangford Lough. Good times, despite the challenges of the year!

On the way home I stopped briefly in Downpatrick where the bones of Saints Patrick, Brigid and Columba are interred. I suddenly remembered that it was in a small gospel hall not far from their grave I first attempted preaching when I was still only a student myself. Now, over thirty years later, I was preparing a sermon on the resurrection for our reopening of public worship.

I'm sure my first sermon all those years ago was pretty clumsy. I didn't know then I would become an ordained church minister. I couldn't foresee all the opportunities for service there have been between then and now. I'm so grateful for hundreds, probably thousands of blessings, seen and unseen, along the way.

While I'm far from being a spiritual giant like Patrick or Brigid, I'm happy to belong in their fellowship, proclaiming to this day the same message of new and eternal life through the crucified and risen Son of God.

None of us saw the Covid-19 pandemic coming or the changes it has brought to the world in 2020. It's a true saying that none of us know what a day, or a year might bring.

Something we might learn to say more often is 'Deo Volente'. 'Deo Volente', usually written shorthand as 'DV', is Latin for 'God willing'. We are wise to recognise higher authority ruling over what happens throughout the world and in our personal circumstances. The apostle James comments, 'Now listen, you who say, "Today or tomorrow we will go to this or that city, spend a year there, carry on business and make money." Why, you do not even know what will happen tomorrow ... Instead you ought to say, "If it is the Lord's will, we will live, and do this or that"' (Jas 4:13–15).

We might all wonder at times exactly why some painful difficulties happen as they do. This has been a hard time and there will doubtless be more challenges to come on the road between now and the day when our Lord will return in glory and God will 'make all things new'. However, we can and should consciously entrust ourselves to the will of the Lord. The future is secure in his love-scarred hands.

As a follower of Jesus Christ, after a lifetime of obeying his plan for me as it has unfolded, I remain thankful to my Shepherd and persuaded of his faithfulness.

Amazing grace has brought us safe thus far.

I believe his grace will lead us safe home.

Why I Do What I Do

Linda Minto

For me, God showed right up during the pandemic. He was here at the start, throughout and at the end, and has stayed right by my side when we were all in lockdown.

I have a company which offers words of comfort, love and hope to others through greeting cards, frames and other products. I work hard at what I do. I lost my own son, Ryan, twenty-four years ago and more than anything I want to offer people words that they will find comfort in. I couldn't find those words when I looked for them to help others, so I started to write those words, right from the bottom of my heart.

I've spent a number of years supplying my stockists – shops that kindly buy my products and spread my words of comfort. But when the pandemic happened, it was inevitable that they would all have to close and go into lockdown too. So I had to think about making my presence online and I did so, without any experience at all. And over time orders started to roll in – quickly reaching demand I had never experienced before. People seemed to be going back to basics, back to love, back to God, to help them in a situation that most of us just could not understand.

When people finally understood the gravity of what was happening, that they couldn't visit their parents, families or friends, it was such a blow to them. Before, life was way too busy to visit in most cases anyway – there always felt like there would be more time – but now that time was taken away just when we needed it more than ever.

As orders rolled in, with them came the telephone calls, more and more frequently as the pandemic continued. People wanted to talk to someone, to tell me why they were ordering the products, what the words on the products meant to them and about the person they were giving them too.

At the start of the pandemic, a young girl from Donegal who had bought some of my Red Robin cards messaged me to say that they had brought so much comfort to her family at a time of absolute crisis. She had lost both her grandparents and an uncle to Covid-19, all within a three-week period. At the time she wrote to me, she also had another two immediate family members in ICU and she didn't know if they would live or die. Thankfully, both lived – one discharged from hospital and one still there as I write this, even after all this time.

We, not as a country but as a world, watched how so much of humanity was affected and the ways in which they dealt with it, from the Italians at the beginning singing to each other from their balconies in the evening to us watching our families look through windows of nursing homes at their loved ones and grandparents raising their hands on window panes to 'feel' just a little touch from the grandchildren that they adored and could no longer hug, kiss or rejoice in.

And yet, there was such an outpouring of understanding from most people, an outpouring of love, an outpouring of giving help to those who needed it, an outpouring of support for the people that had to or chose to put themselves on the frontline to help others – I truly believe that God was working through each and every one of those people.

Another call that stuck with me was from a grandmother whose granddaughter Eleni had sadly passed away. For what must have been an hour we talked about her family's loss as a result of Eleni's death and I talked to her about losing my son, Ryan. I know that we both received so much comfort as a result of that conversation. In times past, I don't believe we would have had that chance. But, during the pandemic, we slowed down, we re-assessed, we took the time to care – and that was when God was with us, showing us what is most important in our lives.

So many other encounters stick in my mind during this pandemic and I was always so grateful to be able to have the time to give to these wonderful, important people. One lady, Terry, called wanting to buy some of my products but didn't have a bank card. She was on her own in her house with no family around her and she was cocooning at the time. She asked if I would accept a postal order if a neighbour would get one for her. It transpired that Terry's husband had died and she had also lost a son and then her daughter soon after. When I received the postal order, it came with a personalised letter from Terry. That letter sits on my desk to this day and will remain there forever as a reminder that my life is blessed and that God introduced us to one another.

As I had received so many calls and messages from people who were buying my products to remember someone that was loved and that had died, I put a cork board in my office and the title I put on it was 'Why I Do What I Do'. On that cork board I place the name of each and every person that someone was remembering when they purchased. When I come down at 6 a.m. each morning, I look at that board and urge myself to keep going on behalf of each and every one of those people. I remember their loved ones and mine and it honestly gives me the push to keep doing what I do. It's absolutely invaluable to me.

So, let me take a step back here and let you know what the pandemic felt like for me. Yes, it was frightening. It was something none of us had ever faced before. But if I'm truthful (and I'm sure I'm in the minority here), there was a part of me that loved it. I truly loved taking a step back from the busyness of life, from the constant demands that are put on us – the chance to just retreat and find myself again and what means the most to me. It gave me the time to re-assess my life in a way that I hadn't had the chance to do in such a long time. Don't get me wrong, I worked from home right throughout the lockdown both on my part-time job and on my own business, so I was really busy, only without the demands of other people on my life.

Of course, I have also experienced the other side of things. As I write this, my gorgeous, wonderful, beautiful and wise dad is currently hospitalised. He's eighty years of age and cannot manage the likes of FaceTime or iPads and the like. He is in a ward, lonely and isolated and unable to move due to being attached to an oxygen tank. Obviously, because of the restrictions, we cannot visit him. He is lonely and down and his days are very long. We are heartbroken not being able to see him. I have so many people praying for him and to get him home to us and I truly believe that God will help us with this. My insight with this has given me a taste of the absolute terror that other people have gone through during this pandemic, losing people closest to them without being able to be there for them, especially in their final hours. Where God has been for us during this time is in the number of people caring about my dad and about us, about the calls, the messages, the reaching out to us with love and care – even the smallest of actions mean so much to us. For anyone reading this that has suffered the pain of losing their loved ones during this pandemic, my heart truly is yours.

At the start of lockdown, I was staying with my mum and dad for a while and one morning I was up before everyone else. I was cooking breakfast and had the back door open and a little red robin appeared on the shed right outside the kitchen door. Anyone who knows me knows that I love the little red robins, so I went and stood at the back door and literally had a chat with the robin. It was such a beautiful moment and it felt like there was only me and that little robin in the world at that time. I turned back to the cooker and all of a sudden the robin flew in through the door and started to walk around the kitchen. Astounded, I turned everything off and sat in my mum's armchair. Lo and behold the little red robin flew up and perched itself on the chair beside me – literally at the height of being able to look into my eyes. I really felt that it was my son who had come to be with me, to tell me that everything would be okay. I sat and chatted to that robin for fifteen to twenty minutes before it took flight and flew out the back door again. It was another way God was present for me during the pandemic.

So where was God in all of your hearts during this time? Have you sat down and reassessed your lives? Have you realised what is most important to you and what is not? Have you decided to live your life in a different way? My part-time job I mentioned earlier is in estate agency and real estate. What I really noticed was that people who had sale agreed on properties before the pandemic suddenly decided that they needed much more space. They didn't want to be in a crowded housing estate, they wanted land that their children could run around on; they wanted to be near people but also have their own space. It's true that things have changed for us all and we've all had to wonder what is important to us. Was that God telling us to re-assess? I really believe so.

The next story I'm about to tell you may sound like poor service from our company, but I truly believe that sometimes things just happen for a reason. I had done up a batch of orders one Sunday afternoon and my son, who was visiting, said that he was heading to his local sorting office the next day and could take them for me. I hesitated but let him go with them. About two weeks later, we sent our usual email: 'You should have received our order by now, can you please give us a review?' One lady answered back and said: 'I would but I haven't received it.' Straight away, I checked all the deliveries I gave to my son and all had been delivered except for this lady's order. I called him and he was adamant that they all had been dropped at the sorting office. Then ten minutes later, I got a call back from him: 'Mam, I'm so sorry, it was in the boot of the car, under the buggy. I missed it!' I actually wondered what to do in the circumstances but at the end of the day, I told her exactly what had happened. She was wonderful about the delay, but the big thing is that when it was sent the next day it actually arrived on the anniversary of her wedding with her first husband. He died when he was thirty-three years of age and she was just twenty-six. She then went on to tell me that three years later she married a man who made her life a misery. I had sent her extra cards as a thank you for being so understanding for our mishap and we formed a strong bond, an understanding that she could talk to me. I truly believe that God orchestrated that encounter so that she had an outlet, someone to talk to who would understand, and I told her as much.

We honestly need to look at the most meaningful aspects of the pandemic, the ways in which the world had to change – we had no choice. My office desk sits at the front window of my house. I have lived here over twenty years and I have never seen so many families out walking or cycling together (in fact, I've never seen so many cyclists in my life!). Families that would never have had the time for such simplicity because life was just busy, busy, busy, with such huge demands placed on all of us. I'm lucky in that we have one of the most beautiful beaches up the road from us. So many people are now going down at sunrise to swim in the sea. This used to happen in small numbers before but now I could drive down at 6 a.m. and see thirty or forty people welcoming the sunrise into their lives while in the sea. What an absolutely beautiful and profound way to start your day. Did being 'locked down' give us the momentum to be free when we could?

My final story is about a wonderful lady who lives in the heart of Dublin City. This lady rang me to order a few cards as her husband had just died. There were many tears on that call. They had two sons, both living in different locations on the other side of the world – neither could get home to bury their much-loved dad and to be with their mam in her time of need. This gorgeous woman was understandably distraught, but it transpired that her neighbours stood right by her side in her hour of need and lined up outside their houses as she brought her lovely husband to his final resting place. She felt their love and their respect for her family and it truly gave her so much comfort. I believe that God travelled with this woman to her beloved husband's final resting place.

My overall assessment of lockdown is that it shook all our lives up in so many ways and made us realise what is truly important to us. Since the pandemic began, I have created a new morning ritual for myself. I rise at 6 a.m. and the very first thing I do is write out at least seven things that I am grateful for. This is such a good start to my day and it truly reminds me of how much I have in life to be thankful for. It had always been on the back of my mind to do this wonderful ritual but, as always, life got in the way. I regularly find myself thanking God for things, things I may not have noticed before: the beautiful sea, the colours of the summer flowers, the sunshine (when we get it!) – there is just so much beauty surrounding us. I won't say I 'found' God during the pandemic because I had always him, it just seems that we have become much closer friends and for that, I am very grateful.

Numbers

A Reflection by John Quinn

They are not
Numbers
Statistics
Worse still, 'part of a trend'.
They were flesh and blood
Our brothers and sisters
For whom Christ died
And rose gloriously.
They were flesh and blood
Who loved and laughed
Lived decent lives
Made people happy
Were bright and productive
Worked and played
And did their best.

They were also liars,
Cheats and charlatans
Who were angry and spiteful,
Said hurtful things
Harboured dark secrets
Were often indifferent,
Cowardly and careless
Of the suffering of others
Too often blind and deaf
And silent.

They were flesh and blood
Just like us
Maybe better, maybe worse
But often, no better nor no worse.
Let them never be
Numbers
Statistics
Or 'part of a trend'.
Let them always be
Our brothers and sisters
Who walked
That Calvary Road,

Simons and Veronicas
Who fell and rose
And fell again
Until they could
Take no more.

And now
Through the risen Christ
Have entered eternal glory.
Rejoicing souls
But never
Numbers

Darkness Gives Light

Maura Walsh OSsR

I recall opening the window of my neatly compact
student room to catch a glimpse of a premature
summer's day infusing my space instantly with
much-needed nurturing air. I had been very
fortunate to have had the opportunity to attend
a study programme on Human Psychospiritual
Development under the guidance of Fr Len Kofler
at St Anselm's Institute, Ciampino, in Rome. It
was February 2020 and, seeking to dissuade
my attention briefly from the complex study of
intrapsychic conflicts, I sought an interlude in
this early summer's breeze. My mind had turned
to the local Italian news, a country now seizing
the world's attention. The cases of the Covid-19
in Northern Italy were starting to make an impact

as the world looked on in silent disbelief at its incredible increasing pace. Weeks passed and the number of deaths climbed rapidly, most severely in the region of Lombardy. Later, towards the end of February, I was made aware from the Irish news updates that the first case of the virus had struck in my very own native Ireland.

Still in Rome, the tensions were rising and as we were multinational students, fears of being unable to return home were imminent. As the death toll continued to rise in Northern Italy many schools, colleges and universities in Rome closed down and students were asked to remain at home. The words 'stay at home and stay safe' were like a new language ushering its way through our corridors and before we could catch a breath our college went into full lockdown. We could not leave the premises and we were informed that there was camera surveillance at all exits so if any of us went outside of the restricted area we would not be allowed back in, as the safety of all was vital.

That summer's breeze had quickly become my avatar searching for its replication within me, needing my attention but I was now elsewhere. At this point in time the focus was on getting me home ahead of the programme's completion date which was in May. The situation was getting worse in both Italy and in Ireland. An overwhelming need to be with your own community or family at a time like this is paramount and for us in Rome the study quickly took second place. Prayer, partnered with logistics, initiated a great effort to get me home early in April, resulting in a number of flights being booked not just in Rome's two airports but also Naples. Naples being further south seemed an understandable choice if all else failed, as there was no guarantee given at all that these flights would actually take place. But on 25 March that I got the call from Srs Gabrielle and Lucy with the near-miraculous news that an Italian Airline was sending a plane over to Dublin to repatriate any Italians that wished to return home which meant it was available to take any Irish that needed to return quickly to Ireland.

The flight booked, I quickly packed and left for Fiumicino airport on the morning of 26 March, along with two Carmelite Sisters from the Tallow community in Co. Waterford who also attended this course: Sr Marie Therese and Sr Kokila. It was a colleague of a resident lecturer that drove us to the airport as taxis were restricted and cautious. I was to travel separately, again, due to cautiousness, and Srs Marie Therese and Kokila together as they were from the one community. I got into that car outside the college reception shrouded in silence once formalities were met. Sanitised, masked up, the college gates slowly opened, and we left. Sitting in the back seat I knew only too well that if this flight was cancelled when we arrived at the airport we could not return to the college as they would not be able to allow us back in. All was well though as we handed over our official 'freedom to travel' letter to the check in desk. Next, we hurried along to board that flight anticipating the isolation that was to greet us, yet reminding ourselves at that moment that it was just our minds that had boarded the plane, our bodies were still very much on Italian soil. We eventually boarded a rather eerie plane that was extremely large with about fifteen passengers, including ourselves, spread out with masks and gloves. The flight attendants kept their distance at all times, but at every opportunity we did our best to convey our appreciation to them through emotion-filled eyes. They knew, they understood.

We all arrived safely at Dublin Airport and I remember so well one of the airport officials, a woman at the passport check point, saying to me 'welcome home', my heart expanded with joy at these two simple words. We arrived back at the monastery soon after that and went into immediate quarantine for two weeks even though we were clear of the virus and had already been in lockdown in Rome for a few weeks. The warmth I felt from my community, even keeping social distance, was so loving and I am eternally grateful to them for getting us back home safely. The very next day, 27 March, the news headlines read that Ireland was going into full lockdown from midnight and all the other flights we were due to take in April were cancelled by the airline. Sisters Marie Therese and Kokila stayed with us for several weeks until some restrictions were lifted, allowing them to return to their own monastery. Where was God in my Italian lockdown? He was on flight AZ241 Alitalia, Departure 16:55, Fiumicino, Rome, Arrival 18:10, Dublin, Ireland. The Italian drama had ended but I continued my lockdown, now in Ireland.

When pondering the question of where God is during these stages of lockdown, we can be sure our blessed Mother Mary is with him. Our Blessed Mother Mary embodies the definition of a true challenge by her 'availability' through her spoken words, 'let it be done unto me'. A acknowledgment of her challenge makes me think, 'what is my challenge during lockdown?' Mary's life was certainly not just a pretty Christmas card story. In her mind alone we find a menu for prayer. In the same way, our vows here as Redemptoristine cloistered nuns are part of the way we change our behaviour. Our 'fiat' is not for ourselves but for the love and will of God in our lives and for the world.

It is from this mode of thinking that I am carried back to my childhood years to thoughts of my dear birth mother, also Mary, now 94, who taught me what the term 'lockdown' meant all those years ago. To lock something down meant to keep something safe, something precious needed to be kept out of harm's way and kept in a trusted place. Returning now to our present pandemic, I believe her words mean the same. On the other hand, an alternative viewpoint on this lockdown is from the French philosopher and atheist, Albert Camus, who died in 1961, calling his last book *The Fall*. Here he used an image to describe people in the world of his time, liking their situation to how prisons were made in the medieval days. In some prisons, boxes were made to put the prisoners in, and these boxes were deliberately built small. Say, for instance, if someone was six foot tall, the prison built the box for this prisoner to only four foot in each direction. The prisoner could never stretch out, stand straight or lie straight. The prison hoped that by doing this it would break the prisoner's spirit, eventually. Today, as lockdown measures have a continued presence in our lives, we can still find ourselves in either of these conditions. But, we can choose to feel that we are being 'kept out of harm's way' or we can choose to feel that our world has become too small for us, leaving us with a 'broken spirit', like the medieval prison.

As I said at the beginning, earlier this year I studied psychospirituality in Rome. Psychospirituality is something that is very much part of our formation here in our monastery. The key to it all is emotions, and it is the negative emotions, much like the medieval prison effect, that sabotage our belief systems in many aspects of our lives. Our dysfunctional beliefs, when unchallenged, will run the show behind the scenes via our subconscious and will control us all the days of our lives. Even the unconscious mind can make an interpretation that it is unsafe, for example, for a memory to be healed, because the purpose of the painful memory is to protect the person from being hurt again! So, when these memories are re-activated, we tend to assign the pain to current circumstances thereby leaving the dysfunctional belief unchallenged. I believe it is true that the biggest trauma we go through is in fact when we are born, coming from our mother's womb. In the natural process of healing that follows we seek comfort and for the first time meet with frustration as our movements are restricted. With that, comes a certain loneliness, an ache, something not always named but we feel it. We feel it again during lockdowns. But we must trust and surrender to God, connecting the psychospiritual's body, mind and spirit with what Jesus said, 'Love the Lord your God with all your heart and with all your soul and with all your mind' (Mt 22:37). In this, I have come to understand that there is a virus that is continually within ourselves, the one that represses our hurtful memories. It is when we put our heart, soul and mind in the medieval prison but convince ourselves that we are just keeping them out of harm's way!

A particular aspect of the lockdown that touched our community deeply were the stories of people not being able to attend the sickbeds and funerals of their loved ones. Our hearts and prayers very much went out to these people but also this was something that would have invoked the memories of some of the sisters here, Sr Michael to name just one. Memories of a time past when, due to the embedded structure of religious life at the time for enclosed nuns, they themselves were not allowed to attend their parent's funerals. Albeit for a very different reason than Covid-19, still the memory causes the same pain. Sr Gabrielle tells of a time earlier in her religious life, not being able to visit her father in hospital before he died. I can only image the grief that must have caused as she recounts the words her father relayed to her about the importance of attending his funeral: 'It is one of the corporal works of mercy.' Prophetic words as this rule has since been changed under the guidance of Sr Gabrielle. Whatever constrains us, whether a virus or law, the pain unites us and, if we choose to be, we are healed.

It is true that our life here as monastics is structured in a way that our enclosure acts for us as a means of deepening our relationship with

God, but, as you can imagine, certain aspects of the lockdown are familiar to our structure. Yet, like everyone else, we were very much affected financially as our altar bread production and sales were reduced drastically to nothing. Nevertheless, our main offering to the suffering world was our constant prayers, and through our webcam we were able to provide daily Mass to many. Eventually thousands were joining us every month from around the world. We continue to share our Mass and prayer life, and we thank God and his Blessed Mother for being with us through it all. I have penned these final words to express our constant assurance of God's light in our darkness:

Corona you covet
but I can see your shield,
masked in hunger for nothing.
You have given us your mask,
we breathe new fear and exhale in isolation.
Death is not your aim
as you travel in un-concrete form,
to evolve your corona reign.

Sculpting a new earth
we have seen despondency
replaced with hygienic control.
We fear the destruction that desires
a will which God has not given breath to.
To us though God has given desire to
    breathe.
and to God it is that our souls do covet.

Small is Beautiful

A Reflection by John Quinn

Stone walls are a prominent feature of the landscape in the west of Ireland. They are obvious examples of the practical use of the environment – clearing the many rocks from the land and using these rocks to mark the boundaries of the fields. They are also works of art in their simple construction, with wonderful features like stiles and 'pooreens' (gaps to allow sheep pass through). Simple in their construction, yes, but simple to construct? Try it sometime! I did some years ago and failed miserably! Before I moved to Clarinbridge, I lived further down the coast in Killeenaran. One day part of my dry-stone garden wall collapsed. I reassembled the wall quite quickly and was feeling proud of my handiwork

– until I barely leaned on it. The whole section came crashing down again. Beginner's ill-luck, I thought, but my second attempt proved equally disastrous. I gingerly made a third reconstruction. Visually it looked fine, but I knew if I breathed heavily on it, it was gone again.

Confused, I sought a neighbour's advice. He took a long-studied look at my effort. 'The secret,' he said eventually, 'is what you do with the small stones'. He proceeded to undo my work – easily done! – and rebuild it, cleverly using the small stones as wedges and holding pieces. 'The small lads are the boys that hold everything together,' he said, seating himself comfortably on the repaired wall.

There's a large moral in that little experience. It's often the small 'unimportant' lads that hold everything together.

A Call to Prayer

Ross Beaton

So many questions have been asked since the beginning of this year, ones which we never expected to have to ask. What is a pandemic? What time is our Zoom later? Do you think I'll be able to meet my friends soon? These are just a sample of some of the questions that we have all become familiar with and have become part of our vernacular this past year.

Life around the world came to a complete standstill shortly after New Year's celebrations in 2020. Little did we know that several months later the world's population would still be trying to assess their lives as they now know them to be. No doubt the end of year reviews on television and radio will look somewhat different compared to those gone by. There is one question that seemed to be absent from many peoples' thoughts and that is 'Where is God in all of this?' It is a question that I have not heard much in the past seven months and it's not something I thought much about myself until recently. Why is this? Have I been too obsessed with the news and media to even focus on God? Have I neglected my faith throughout this pandemic, a time when I, and perhaps the whole world, probably needed to focus on faith more than ever? These are the thoughts I have been faced with recently, and I am probably not alone in that. I want to try and explore this question and delve into the actual meaning of the presence of God in my life, a life based in a country where Christianity is not the primary faith but is nonetheless present and freely practised.

I came across a quote recently which I believe was extremely relevant for people this year. 'Our hurting world is plagued by challenges that can't be overcome unless we bring big heart and our best selves to confront the world's ills'.[1] The world is both literally and metaphorically ill right now.

The pandemic has swept the globe and taken so many people with it, but we as a community are also hurt, angry and dejected about all that we have been through.

Before I go any further, let me give you some information as to my perspective on all of this. I am a twenty-seven-year-old English and religion teacher from Rathfarnham, Dublin, who moved to the United Arab Emirates in February 2019. Islam is the primary religion practised here but the freedom and expression of all faiths is allowed and even encouraged. The UAE is a country filled with beautiful culture, food and, of course, the most amazing weather. It is a country nestled in the Arabian Gulf and is a nation of freedom and generosity. In fact, the year I arrived was designated as the 'Year of Tolerance'. This was an opportunity for people to learn about each other, for children in schools to be educated about the world around them and the many nationalities that live in the UAE. Just before I moved out here, Pope Francis made a historic visit to the country which was celebrated by all.

God is certainly present in the UAE and there is pride for all who are Muslim. One of the most striking things I noticed throughout lockdown when I was in my apartment working from home was the call to prayer. This is a daily ritual which occurs five times a day for Muslims and is sounded through the speakers of the local mosque. The call to prayer reminds worshippers to pray at the prescribed times throughout the day. Although some may see it as unnecessary, I found myself listening to the sound of the prayer and the chanting melody of it each day despite the fact that I can't understand Arabic. I would stop for the couple of minutes it lasted and just recognise that God is present not only for Muslims, but for the entire world. This ritual that would wake me early in the morning became something I appreciated as a reminder of the deep sense of faith that existed in our world.

When the initial stringent lockdown was eased I started to resume my exercises of walking or running around the local park which was a tranquil and relaxing experience (despite the high temperatures and humidity!). Along my route, I arrived at the local mosque, which is called Mary the Mother of Jesus Mosque and directly adjacent to it is St Joseph's Cathedral, Abu Dhabi. I discovered the cathedral when I first moved here and have been a regular attendee of Masses and other celebrations. Large crowds would gather every Sunday and it surprised me how popular it was amongst local residents and those from further afield. For obvious reasons the cathedral has been closed since the beginning of lockdown, but this has not deterred people from visiting it on a daily basis. Passing the cathedral I would always see a dozen or so people scattered and socially distanced from one another surrounding the gates. They were cherishing and adoring the architecture of this scared place. Just like the call to prayer, it was a true sign of the presence of God. I would often stop myself, just to stand and distract myself from all those around me and the cacophony of noises coming from the streets behind me and just pray. It was the most simple of exercises but there was something so profound about a community made up of various nationalities, ages and races coming to these walls and just stopping. There has always been a perception that the heart of a church or a cathedral is inside but I believe throughout lockdown this had been turned outwards, creating a symbol of recognition and reiterating the presence of God in our lives.

The question about the presence of God this year can also be phrased in a more theological and existential sense as opposed to the presence of God in our everyday lives. Where is God? A question that has meant so much more to millions of people around the world before the pandemic this year. Liberation theology deals with the concept of the oppressed and vulnerable in our world and why they endure so much hardship and desperation in their life. The root of this question goes beyond the vulnerable and oppressed and can be linked to the whole human race and the Christian family.

As I write this reflection I am viewing some of most horrific and abhorrent sights from Beirut in Lebanon. No matter the cause or effect of this tragic crisis, I can't help but ask myself, where is God? Why would an all-loving, omnipresent God let such a damaging and destructive event take place for his people? My thoughts on this go right back to the pandemic and the shift in our lives to what has been referred to as the 'new normal'. Has God been present with us since this all began? Is this a reminder to us all, to stop and take stock of our lives and the world around us? I cannot deny that I have become more aware of the nature that surrounds me and my home, the beautiful park and it's flourishing foliage, the immaculate and rich beaches, the delicious food that I have cooked and experimented with and, most importantly, my connection with family and friends. As I look back now, I firmly believe this was the presence of God in my life. I have undoubtedly appreciated the smaller, more precious things in life over these past few months. Most important, however, is the realisation that these are the only things we need in life.

I am very fortunate to work and live with such a welcoming and loving Irish community – one that is not only present where I live, but also across the city and even further afield. At times like these you begin to realise who your true friends are and there has been plenty of time for reflection about our relationships with those around us, but also with those we may have lost contact with. When St Paul wrote to the Corinthians he simply said, 'faith, hope and love; and the greatest of these is love' (1 Cor 13:13). It's as simple as that.

A number of my friends suffered terrible losses during lockdown – some Covid-19 related, others not. The frustration of not being able to travel and spend time with family was an unimaginable thought for so many of us and it really magnified the importance of having one another. You often hear the phrase 'God works in mysterious ways' and I truly believe this is true. Some may see it as contradiction to the earlier question of his presence but if you believe and are steadfast in your faith, it will see you through. For my friends and I, it may have been making someone a cup of tea, surprising them with a treat, or simply sending a message or knocking on the door. This was the presence of God during lockdown.

In Matthew's gospel, Jesus talks about living the best life that we can as Christians. The words are striking yet simple and very much relevant today: 'Therefore do not worry about tomorrow, for tomorrow will worry about itself. Each day has enough trouble of its own' (Mt 6:34). The basis for all of this is love and the vital necessity of surrounding ourselves with the right people to guide us through life and fulfil our best potential.

A couple of months ago I came across a thought-provoking question Fr William A. Barry SJ asks in his book *Praying the Truth*: 'When you are with a friend and are riddled with fear, what else do you have to talk about that's important?'[2] Take a moment to yourself and ponder that question. What does it say to you, and how can you relate this to the presence of God in your life, with a focus on the past few months? For many young people fear and anxiety has been an overwhelming constant in their lives, myself included. The pandemic was no different and certainly exacerbated any underlying or hidden fears that so many young people in the world have today. This is something that has really struck me in the past few months. Perhaps it is the teacher and natural observer in me but there has been a shift in the mentality of young people since lockdown began and for me this is where the true question of the presence or dare I say the absence of God has lived.

As people have had more time on their own and have been cooped up in their own space, many have formed an unhealthy reliance on social media. Before I go any further, I am a great advocate for social media and the wondrous benefits it offers to people, especially for connecting with those abroad or at home, but there can be negative aspects as well. There is a need in young people today to want and have everything that someone else has and to look like them because they are living a so-called 'perfect life', but where is God here? Is he present when you are having these thoughts and feelings that are predicated on minor fear, but then develop into something more concerning that results in self-loathing, isolation and paranoia towards those around you? The rise in mental health cases throughout lockdown has been staggering and there are, of course, many reasons for individual cases, but for young people it has been a precarious time and a lack of faith and even simple conversations with friends or family members signals the absence of God for so many people. Saint Paul, in another profound letter, this time to the Philippians, wrote, 'Do nothing out of selfish ambition or vain conceit. Rather, in humility value others above yourselves' (Phil 2:3–4). It is important to note that enjoying social media is not a sin or anything to be condemned, but rather that social media should serve as a tool for connecting with people and discovering the world. I myself am guilty of indulging in social media, television and shopping, but there comes a time when you have to stop. Realising what's truly important is vital and praying for a moment with the presence of God connects the mind and soul once again with real life.

Just the other day I was chatting to a friend of mine over a coffee and, as with most of our conversations over the past few months, we arrived at the junction of the pandemic and lockdown. As humans we are naturally inclined to think, to worry, to wonder. It is in our nature. It is safe to say that the past few months have been life changing for so many people and it really has altered the landscape of the world that we live in. I said to my friend that we are so focused on the negative aspects of life and what goes wrong, but what about the positive aspects? Take an exam for example. You always remember and isolate what you got wrong or could not remember as opposed to all the questions you got right. Lockdown is similar, though of course on a much more serious scale. Take a moment to think about this concept, however.

As my friend and I were chatting I said to him that we are on a pilgrimage of hope. Yes, hope. It may sound strange and not realistic but we are now living in a time when we need it more than ever. Hope for all healthcare workers that they will be justified and lauded for their miraculous work; hope for communities to come together and be resilient in the face of adversity; hope for young people that they see the value in their loved ones and in all they have; hope for the elderly and vulnerable in society that they are not neglected or forgotten about in the future. There is hope and we have to continue this pilgrimage and follow God's presence because he is with us. 'And surely I am with you always, to the very end of the age' (Mt 28:20).

ENDNOTES

1   Chris Lowney, *Make Today Matter: 10 Habits for a Better Life (and World)*, Chicago: Loyola Press, 2018.

2   William A. Barry SJ, *Praying the Truth*, Chicago: Loyola University Press, 2012, p. 29.

Everything Passes

A Reflection by John Quinn

Some years ago, I was asked to give a talk in St Kieran's College, Kilkenny – no, not on how to produce hurlers, they don't need any advice on that! – on writing, as it happened.

As I entered the college grounds. I noticed an inscription carved in stone above the gate: *Hiems Transiit*. Having been a decent Latin scholar during my own schooling, I could translate this straight away as 'Winter Has Passed', but I was puzzled as to its significance. I subsequently discovered it was the school's motto.

Saint Kieran's was founded in 1782, after the passing of the Relief Act of that year which enabled Catholics to set up schools. 'Winter' was a metaphor for the Penal Laws, which had deprived them of such liberties for the best part of a century. It had truly been a long winter, but it had passed. As all things do, if only we have patience.

We rail against the harshness of our own winters, whether it be severe weather conditions or an 'economic' winter of austerity brought on by a recession or even a virus, but they will pass. John O'Donohue liked to tell of a contest that was held in ancient Greece to find a sentence that would somehow always be true. The winning sentence was 'This too will pass'. John further quoted St Teresa of Ávila, who said that no matter how difficult or lonesome times may be, we should be consoled by the knowledge that these too will pass. It may be very difficult when we are in the middle of those times, but we trust in the goodness of the Lord.

So, be it weeks of ice and snow, centuries of Penal Laws, an economic recession or a seemingly endless pandemic, 'winter' will always pass. It is written in stone.

Music – My Companion

Marie Dunne CHF

For me, my music, faith and life are intertwined. I have never known a time when music didn't play a significant role in my life. Over the years, music has nourished my faith, and my faith has inspired my music.

From when I was a young child, there is no time in my life when this wonderful 'companion' was not by my side. My grandmother introduced me to my 'five finger exercises' when I was five years old. There was always lots of music in our home with both of my parents sharing a great interest in and love for music. When I was seven, I started formal piano lessons at the Holy Faith Convent, Killester, where I went to school. I was taught by a wonderful lady – Sr Mary Declan. Her encouragement and interest in me, and in my music journey, deepened my love for something that would become one of the strongest influences in my life.

As a musician and a composer of sacred and spiritual music, I have been privileged to share special moments with so many, and to use this God-given gift in a variety of ways. I have been enriched by those I have journeyed with, in and through music. I have come to realise that music indeed is a language unto itself – a language of the heart. It can unite us and connect us in the deepest of ways that bring us into the heart of God. I pray that I will always be grateful for the privilege of being able to share God's love and my faith through my gift of music.

As we know, music touches us at the deepest part of our heart. I quote from a song I composed some years ago, 'Journey to Your Heart':

The journey to the heart will bring you to
    that place
Where you will find your deepest peace,

Find the path the leads you to that sacred
   place,
Find the way that leads you to me.

For me, music has so often brought me to a
deep place in my heart, where I have experienced
God's presence and love. It is from that deep
experience that I want to share not only my music,
but the love God has for each of us. In my music
compositions, I endeavour to reflect hope and
trust, especially when life is grim and dark. I try
to echo this in songs such as *Before the Dawning*
(the song composed for Saint Francis Hospice
20th anniversary in 2009.) This message of
hope is also found in the song *A Candle for You* to
remember missing persons. The final words read:

I live in hope for I believe
The sun will rise again.

The above reflection has been written at
a time when our world is living through the
Covid-19 pandemic. This is a difficult time for

so many. Once again we are challenged to draw on our inner strengths of faith, hope and love. During this pandemic I have been able to spend a lot of time with the companion I dare to call 'my music' – a companion who has never left my side. I have been able to share in a visual way much of music on YouTube and other platforms. It is my deepest wish and desire to share God's comfort and love through the channel with which I have been gifted and blessed: my faith and my music. As I reflect on my music's journey, it is not me that brought my music on a journey, but my music that has guided me to so many places only to find the presence of God waiting there. I conclude with words from my album of scriptural chants entitled *Shelter Me*. May these words offer us hope and reassurance in these times.

Shelter me O God, shelter me O God,
Keep me safe in your love.
Shelter me from storms that pass along the
way,
Shelter me, shelter me O God.

Protection

A Reflection by John Quinn

In our present circumstances, there is much concern with the need for protection. It pleases me greatly to join daily with Fr Barry and the community in reciting that lovely prayer for protection known as 'St Patrick's Breastplate'. It is such a comforting and reassuring prayer.

> Christ within me, Christ before me, Christ behind me …

A long time ago at school we learned how St Patrick had incurred the wrath of King Laoire when he lit the paschal fire on the Hill of Slane. The king summoned Patrick to Tara next day to explain his actions. But the druids, who were even more fearful than the king, set out to ambush and kill Patrick and his followers as they made their way to the royal palace.

As the Druids waited, they heard chanting from the approaching group. Soon they could discern the words …

Christ on my right hand, Christ on my left …

This was *Lúireach Phadraig* – St Patrick's Breastplate – a shield that no human weapon could pierce. The assailants were mystified, even more so when all they could see passing was a herd of deer. The miraculous disguise and the lengthy chant ensured that Patrick and his company reached Tara safely.

It's a fanciful tale, but a rather wonderful one. The chant or hymn became known as 'The Deer's Cry'. Over fifteen centuries later, in a Midlands boarding school, I would recite that hymn together with my fellow-students at the end of our night prayers in the school oratory …

Christ in every eye that sees me, Christ in every ear that hears me …

For we were under the care of the Patrician Brothers, so it was our Breastplate too – even if we struggled with some of the dated language …

Christ in the fort, Christ in the chariot, Christ on the ship …

So now, another sixty years later, I am delighted to join once more in the recitation of the Breastplate for our communal protection. In my mind, I rewrite some of the lines to reflect the times that are in it …

Christ in the hearts of those who shop for me …
Christ in the hands of those who bake and cook meals for me …
Christ in the minds of those who call and text and send cards to let me know they are thinking of me …

I give thanks for the many ways I am not just protected but am nourished and truly blessed.

Covid-19 – A Reflection

Martin (Jarlath) Gormally

Another night, another dawn,
Another day of draining dread,
Will our loved one still be here?
We hope and pray.

Listed as lately deceased,
Statistics do not tell
Of Mary, John, or Baby Nell,
Mother, Pop, or sibling Ben,
Loved by family and by friends.
Impersonal figures, cold and bleak,
Bring no relief.

Nightly tallies we await,
Conscious of impending fate

Of one whose life we celebrate.
High renown, those once of fame,
Who survives? Who shares the blame?

Infection rising in the state,
Hospitals bulge to accommodate.
Why did we fail to heed the news?
As patients joined the lengthy queues
While we, with little thought, each day,
Continued on our heedless way.

A sealed bag – a numbered tag
Through which no face or eye can peep,
No wake, no dirge, no trumpet call,
No stories told or pipers play,
To lead our loved one on their way!

Scientists tell us, 'Be prepared!'
This virus will not go away.
Follow what our experts say,
'Desperate diseases', the wise assured,
'By desperate remedies must be cured'.

Preventive vaccine, ray of hope,
The vulnerable first to take,
Aged, infirm, will all partake,
And doctors, nurses, in front-line role,
Risk infection and take the toll.

Preventive measures, are prescribed,
Hand wash, face masks, quarantine,
Obey the rules, harsh though they be,
For if adopted universally,
Will play a part in the virus fight,
Do it now, to get it right.

This is my one and final plea!
It's up to you, it's up to me.

Loss and Grief

A Reflection by John Quinn

For each of us there are dates that stand out in our memory. They are significant milestones in our lives. For me, 1 March 1966 was the day I first laid eyes on a beautiful, elegant woman. Her name was Olive McKeever. On 18 September 1968 we were married. I felt so proud and privileged. But 25 June 2001 is the date that has burned itself into my memory. On that date Olive died suddenly, before my eyes, while swimming in the sea at Rosslare. So, as 25 June approaches once more, I reflect on loss and grief.

Nothing can prepare you for the loss of a loved one – especially a sudden loss. You are totally numb. The goalposts have been moved. A part of you has gone. Life will never be the same again.

The great dark cloud of grief envelops you. It cuts very deep and leaves you very raw. Grief is, however, natural and necessary. It enfolds the loved one in fond recollection. It is the ultimate marker of love for the lost one. John O'Donohue tells us that though the grief journey is slow, you will come through its great valley into a meadow where light and colour and promise await to embrace you. You so want to believe that, but in the early days it is very hard.

And then grief is often accompanied by regret. If only I had said (or hadn't said) that; if only I had done (or hadn't done) that. A neighbour said to me at the time, 'I have no time for this regret stuff. If you didn't travel the road you travelled, you wouldn't be where you are now.' Very Irish and very true, but we are human and we do regret … And then there's time. Time is 'the great healer', we are told. 'You'll be grand', we are told. Not so! Time does help you to accommodate, but as Joan Wilson, widow of peace campaigner Gordon Wilson, said, 'The wound is always there.' And often it takes very little to open it. Time does bring consolations, however, and the greatest of these is memory – often the memory of seemingly unimportant trivial things. That's not to say that a marriage of thirty-three years is all sunshine and roses. In every relationship there are ups and downs. There were the times of what Olive called 'deep freezes', when nobody was talking to anybody for days! But, to use J.M. Barries' lovely phrase, 'God gave us memory so that we might have roses in December.' So it's important to cherish the memory of happy moments.

And memory begets gratitude. I am extremely grateful to the Lord and to Olive for our life together and for the blessings we enjoyed – despite the deep freezes!

In the end, the great consolation is hope. I am convinced I will meet Olive again. The how and the where and the when is all mystery. I can only rely on the words of the Dutch priest Henri Nouwen, who says we just need to be patient. These are his words: 'All will be well. How? Do not ask. Why? Do not worry. Where? You will know. Just wait quietly, peacefully, joyfully. All will be well.'

Diary of a Homeless Man

Glenn Gannon

As a homeless advocate and homeless ambassador for the Dublin Simon Community for twenty years, I have given talks to almost every secondary school and college in Dublin and its environs. I not only talk about homelessness, but also about topics that the teachers often cannot really discuss in great detail, such as suicide or alcohol and drug dependency. They are tricky subjects, but the teachers always say they are glad I touched on them in as light a way as possible.

'How do you know so much about homelessness?' a student invariably asks. To which I reply, 'Because I was homeless for over three years.' Then the room usually becomes silent. So I tell them I'm not embarrassed by it.

It happened for many reasons, but it happened, and I had to work very hard to escape from the black hole of depression that is homelessness is.

'How do you stay positive?' a student asked me one time. Well, when you spend your days wandering around the city with long hair and a beard you become invisible and so you bed down in laneways and suffer all that life and the weather can throw at you. But no matter where I had tried to sleep the night before I always awoke with a prayer of gratitude on my lips. Gratitude for waking at all, as life on the streets is very short. So, I would pray to God and thank him for another day in which I could try to make my life a bit better and thank him for blessing and protecting my family who were young at the time. The pain of not seeing them was sometimes unbearable, so I would drink cheap wine to try to forget, and pretty soon I couldn't remember what it was I was trying to forget.

I used to sit outside the chapel at John's Lane and the Mass-goers all knew me and would talk with me. I would tell them I was going to write a book. Some would laugh and wish me well. I blessed them all and they would put Miraculous Medals around my neck. There was my positivity. There was my God. In all these kind souls, I found loving hearts and caring eyes that looked upon me with real affection. They were my comfort sent to me by God. I truly believe that. My most treasured moments were when the chapel was empty. I would sit quietly at the back of the church because I felt I was not worthy to sit near the blessed statues, and I would quietly pray. I eventually got off the streets and, with the help of Sr Consillio, got sober and set about writing that book, which became *Miracle Man: From Homeless to Hollywood*. It is my pride and joy, not because it is a learned book – it's not – but because it proves to the world that with a little faith in God as small as a mustard seed you can move mountains.

My dad was a great man for debates when we were young. You could ask him anything and he could speak knowledgably on any subject. 'Where was God?' the world asked after the Second World War. Over seven million Jews were slaughtered at the hands of the Nazi war machine, and millions more of many nationalities also lost their lives. The straight answer to that has to be that God was in the camps with the condemned. Great stories of heroism and self-sacrifice emerged with the liberation of the death camps. My father, though an Irish citizen, was one of the British soldiers who actually went into those camps, and for the rest of his life he suffered terrible trauma from what he had seen. As an inquisitive young boy, I would ask him about the camps and he could not bear to discuss it. He would tell me of his exploits as a tank man in North Africa but he would not speak of the horrors of Auschwitz and Bergen-Belsen. His eyes would fill with tears and he would bless himself.

When I became a young man and had done my own research, I tried in vain again to broach the subject and again his eyes would fill up and he would only nod to say no. I told my dad that I believed that God was in the camps. My more learned and mostly atheistic friends would challenge me when the subject would arise: 'Why do you believe that God was in the camps?' I told them, 'Because where else would Jesus be but amongst the innocent and the condemned?' For was Christ himself not innocent and was Christ not condemned and did he not suffer hours of agony and torment upon that cross? Where else would he be then but praying with them as the hour of their death approached, just as he himself had prayed in the Garden of Gethsemane.

Wherever there is suffering and tragedy, there you will find Jesus of Nazareth. It must be so. It cannot be any other way. If you look at the saints throughout history, they almost all suffered. All Christ's disciples bar one died horrible deaths. 'Why?' my friends ask. My answer is simple: look to the life and death of Christ and his apostles. Jesus was condemned. Jesus was tortured. Jesus was tried, convicted and crucified. Where did the disciples go? They ran away. They hid in an upstairs room that was bolted shut. They were terrified. All the gospels agree that this is what happened. And rightly so. Their leader was dead. The romans and the Sanhedrin and all their spies were looking for the disciples to kill all of them to quell this new religion. Why then did these twelve scared men suddenly decide to throw open the doors of their only sanctuary against certain death to go out into the streets and proclaim that Jesus was alive and that they had seen him? Logic dictates that Jesus was amongst them when they were suffering and made himself known to them physically. He let them see and touch his wounds. This is not idle guesswork; this is documented in the Bible. Every one of those disciples no longer feared death. Why? Because they had seen death conquered by the risen Christ.

How can we be sure of this? Twenty-first century people demand proof. So, when I do my school talks as a homeless advocate across every school in Dublin I give them proof. Jesus said of Doubting Thomas, 'You believe because you have seen me and touched my wounds. Blessed are they who have not seen and believe.' The proof I speak of to this generation can be found on Google or YouTube. There exists a piece of linen that is housed in the Turin Cathedral. It is without a doubt the shroud of a crucified man of about thirty years of age. He is taller than the men from Jerusalem and surrounding areas by a good few inches at a height of five foot, ten inches. The lines show that his back was heavily shredded and his five wounds include a piercing from a lance. His eyes were closed by coins the outlines of which are clearly visible. They show a man's head and bear the inscription *'Tiberius Caesar'*. which places this man in the time of Tiberius's reign as emperor, the exact time of Christ's death. There are wounds to his head caused by thorns from a plant which was only available in the area of Judea. Proof of this was found in pollen still contained in the face cloth covering the face of this man. So here we have a tall man who was tortured, crucified, killed with a lance and had a crown of thorns placed on his head and the image which is only visible through the negative of a photograph. It is not painted onto the surface of the shroud but is scorched onto it by an internal force of great power to cause the imprint. *Ecce Homo*.

All of this evidence should be enough to convince even the harshest critic of the presence of Jesus of Nazareth not only in the upper room of that house after the crucifixion of Christ but in our everyday lives. Right now, he is in the ICUs of the world as some poor person struggles to breathe. He is whispering prayers and words of comfort to those struggling for breath as the coronavirus steals the life from their lungs. He is omnipotent. He is omniscient. He is omnipresent. He is in the heart of the pandemic. He is comforting the broken hearted. He is carrying children to heaven. His is the last voice that they hear. But it surely comforts us all to know that he is with us through this terrible time. For did Jesus not tell us, 'Be not afraid. I go before you always. Come, follow me, and I will give you rest.'

Peace be to you.

Being Brave

A Reflection by John Quinn

The recent death of Jean Kennedy Smith brought to mind the role she played in the staging of the Special Olympic World Summer Games in Dublin in 2003. It was an unforgettable week of pride, pageantry and participation.

The swimming competitions were held in the National Aquatic Centre. In one heat of the 15 Meter Unassisted Swim competition there are only three competitors. Each has an assistant following in the water in case of emergency. A boy from the Seychelles Islands wins the heat easily in 14.7 seconds. A boy from Honduras comes second in 17.97 seconds. All eyes turn to the third competitor. She is Hazel Zumbado, aged fifteen, from Costa Rica. She is deaf and mute and out of the water she is confined to a wheelchair, but she has the use of her arms and so can swim. She takes a long time to get going and the crowd responds to her huge effort. Frank McNally caught the moment in his *Irish Times* report:

> They're are shouting, screaming, urging her every inch of the way. Her progress is measured in inches, as enormous effort translates into tiny advances through the water ... There are now four assistants in the water, encouraging and ready to help if needed. But the swimmer is going to make it without their assistance, and with everyone in the packed gallery on his or her feet, applauding, she touches the wall in 1 minute 59.23 seconds.[1]

How beautifully Hazel epitomised the Special Olympic Games motto: 'Let me win, but if I cannot win let me be brave in the attempt.' In the present time, we all need some of Hazel's bravery.

ENDNOTES

1   Frank McNally, 'One Small and Determined Girl Makes a Big
     Splash with the Gallery', *Irish Times*, 26 June 2003.

When You Come Out of the Storm

Megan McKenna

When you come out of the storm, you won't be the same person who walked in.[1]

A storm! It's a good image to describe the last six months, the onslaught of the Covid-19 pandemic and its spread like a wild fire across the world. It is a furious storm with waves of suffering and death, winds that are headlong and gusting, affecting not only our bodies but our spirits and our souls.

There are two stories in the gospel about storms. The first is found in the Gospel of Matthew (14:22–36):

Then he made the disciples get into the boat and precede him to the other side, while he dismissed the crowds. After doing so, he went up on the mountain by himself to pray. When it was evening he was there alone. Meanwhile the boat, already a few miles offshore, was being tossed about by the waves, for the wind was against it. During the fourth watch of the night, he came toward them, walking on the sea. When the disciples saw him walking on the water they were terrified. 'It is a ghost', they said, and they cried out in fear. At once Jesus spoke to them, 'Take courage; it is I. Do not be afraid.' Peter said to him in reply, 'Lord, if it is you, command me to come to you on the water.' He said, 'Come!' Peter got out of the boat and began to walk on the water toward Jesus. But when he saw how strong the wind was he became frightened and, beginning to sink, he cried out, 'Lord, save me!' Immediately Jesus stretched out his hand and caught him, and said to him, 'O you of little faith, why did you doubt?' After they got into the boat, the wind died down. Those who were in the boat did him homage, saying, 'Truly, you are the Son of God.'

This is us; cowering in a boat, buffeted against water and wind all night until the fourth watch (between 3 a.m. and 5 a.m.), fearing for our lives. It is thought that the disciples did not know how to swim and the storms that would come up without warning were treacherous with winds strong enough to flip their boats. They are exhausted physically but the strain has been heightened by their fears not only of death but of so many other things that rise to the surface when we are faced with danger and our own mortality.

Jesus comes to them, walking on the water. They saw him through the driving wind and rain, waves swamping their boat, being thrown up and down, and in their state of mind they think they are seeing a ghost. Jesus speaks to them words of assurance, 'Take courage; it is I. Do not be afraid.'

These are the same words to describe God in the earlier testament! And Peter, ever impulsive and rash, says: 'If it is you, command me to come to you across the water.' And Jesus simply says: 'Come!' And probably without thinking, Peter gets out of the boat (not easy to do at any time, but more so in the midst of a storm). And to his shock, finds himself walking on the top of the waves, moving towards Jesus.

A few steps in and he begins to realise what's going on all around him, what he is actually doing (something impossible and unnatural) and the boat receding behind him and his attention is pulled away from Jesus. He takes his eyes off of him. And, like someone walking a tightrope who looks back or down, losing their balance, he sinks. His physical fear swamps him as the waves rise up and he cries out: 'Lord, save me.' And Jesus stretches out his hand, grasps a hold of him and hauls him upright. Jesus goes fishing and reels him in! Together they turn and head back towards the boat. Did they go arm in arm; or was Jesus dragging him, still in shock? And it's no easy thing to get back into the boat. And then, in a moment, it is quiet; all is stilled. It is the calm after the storm.

There is where we are today: in a boat crowded with many other frightened people enduring the storm of a pandemic.

Author Arundhati Roy wrote:

Historically, pandemics have forced humans to break with the past and imagine their world anew. This one is no different. It is a portal, a gateway between one world and the next. We can choose to walk through it, dragging the carcasses of our prejudices and hatred, our avarice, our data banks and dead ideas, our dead rivers and smokey skies behind us. Or we can walk through lightly, with little baggage, ready to imagine another world. And ready to fight for it.[2]

Now we have a taste of how to live in the storm and after. Storms not only destroy, they also scatter what needs to be cleared away, leaving us space to make new paths. What does this look like? How do we restore balance, recreate our lives, repair our battered society and our individual souls?

There is an ancient Japanese art form called 'kintsukuroi', also called 'kintsugi'. It has been practised for nearly five hundred years. When an object that is worth a small fortune such as a vase, a cup or a bowl, etc., is broken and shattered into pieces, it is brought to an artist to be repaired. It is a painstaking and delicate task requiring finely honed skills. The artist puts the item back together again, concentrating on the spaces between the broken pieces and shards. These thin and jagged spaces are filled with liquid gold or silver lacquer so that when the materials dry the restored piece is a thing of surpassing beauty, now priceless. This is the art we all must practise with one another, on all the institutions, structures, laws and ways in our society, and even more delicately, tenderly and patiently on each other's bodies, psyches, spirits and souls. The cracks will remain, but they will form the foundation of what will change and make something whole and more exquisite.

We are being given two gifts. The first, the gift of crisis. The root of the word in Greek means to sift, to shake loose from excess and leave behind only what is essential. Crises force us to decide what we will grasp and hold onto and what we will pry ourselves away from; keeping what matters most and leaving all else behind as detritus.

The second gift is the chance to make our fears our friends! In the gospel passage Jesus is in the storm, as he is in all things. And he 'commands' us to come towards him, to walk on the water and to live his way with daring as an adventure that can save us!

It is told in a Jewish Midrash that when Moses and the people got to the Red Sea, with the Egyptian army right behind them, they were dismayed at the wall of water that confronted them. Moses insisted that they move forward, stretching out his staff over the water. But it is said that no one moved, they screamed in fear, paralysed, crying and praying for God to save them. And then one person dove into the water, and immediately the waters started to move and as the person sought to swim, their feet found footing on ground and the way opened up before them. Then, and only then, did the others plunge into the moving thrashing waters and walked through the sea that parted before them to freedom. Jesus tells Peter, and all of us: 'O you of little faith, why did you doubt?' It is time for us to plunge in.

The second storm story of the gospels is found in the Gospel of Mark (4:36–41):

On that day, as evening drew on, he said to them, 'Let us cross over to the other side.' Leaving the crowd, they took him with them in the boat just as he was. And other boats were with him. A violent squall came up and the waves were breaking over the boat, so that it was already filling up. Jesus was in the stern, asleep on a cushion. They woke him and said to him, 'Teacher, do you not care that we are perishing?' He woke up, rebuked the wind, and said to the sea: 'Quiet! Be still!' The wind ceased and there was great calm. Then he asked them, 'Why are you afraid? Do you not have faith?' They were filled with great awe and said to one another, 'Who then is this whom even wind and sea obey?'

This is how we have often felt during these long months: In the boats, in the storm – and God may be with us, but he's asleep! And so our prayer is often frantic and distressed: 'Wake up, God! Don't you care that we're perishing?' Author Isabel Allende has said: 'We all have an unsuspected reserve of strength inside that emerges when life puts us to the test.'[3] And this reserve is also what we used to call 'actual' grace that is given in every instance as we need it. The storm calls us to discover this grace within ourselves and calls us forth, commanding us to use that strength to obey the gospel, and together to transform our realities. The oceanographer Jacques-Yves

Cousteau once said: 'The sea, the great unifier, is man's only hope. Now, as never before, the phrase has a literal meaning: we are all in the same boat.'[4] We are all in the same storm on the same seas. Though, as the scripture says, 'other boats were with him'. Our God is with us. His presence is both a comfort and the power to survive, to live with enduring grace and rely on his word and one another to weather this storm and all the other storms and fears that are surfacing in the midst of the massive changes and radical uncertainties surrounding this virus in our lives. But Jesus' words are good news, words of hope, freedom and liberation. Sharing them is a way to keep in touch communicating with one another, feeding our fears on hope rather than letting our fears eat away at our faith.

The essayist Rebecca Solnit has said that 'Hope locates itself in the premises that we don't know what will happen and that in that spaciousness of uncertainty is room to act.'[5] This pandemic throws us overboard, out of 'what was normal' and into mystery and wild possibilities for a future transformed by our experiences. We are now (hopefully) learning compassion; justice; concern for the poor; connection to all peoples, even to the world and earth's elements of air, wind, fire and water; and a sense of mutual reciprocity, intimacy and sheer necessity of all existence binding us together as the foundation that we need to rebuild and repair.

When I spent a good deal of time in Latin America and stayed with families, I was often given a gift the first night I slept in their house. Usually it was one or more of the children that came to me in their nightshirts when I was getting settled on the straw, or in someone else's borrowed bed. They were giggling and would hand me a tiny box, no bigger than three to four inches, often smaller. It was often made of straw woven together, painted red, green, yellow and whatever colors they could mix. They would tell me to take the top off. Inside were tiny dolls, intricately made, dressed to look like all of them – sometimes four or five, more often as many as there were people sharing the house we were in.

They told me solemnly that they were 'worry' dolls. I was to take them out, line them up and tell each one of them a worry, a concern, something or someone I was thinking about. And then once I'd told it to one of them, put it back in the box. Then when all my troubles, sadness and worries were in the box, put the top back on and put it beside my bed. Then I could go to sleep easily and the dolls would keep my troubles for me and I could face them tomorrow morning with fresh eyes and rest.

It is a good way to face each night these months. Get a small box with some stones. You can tell your troubles, fears and worries to the stones and put them in the box, or tell them to God to keep them overnight. Lay them aside and go to bed, sleeping next to Jesus already asleep in the boat with us. God will still our hearts and give us rest and, like the disciples, we will find that our fears have become awe before our God and that we are loved, protected and saved every moment. When we sleep and dream with God, we rise to ride out the storms and learn to walk on water, secure, knowing our God has hold of us and dwells with us. Come! In every moment: 'Take courage; it is I. Do not be afraid.'

ENDNOTES

1   Haruki Murakami, *Kafka on the Shore*, New York: Vintage International, 2006.

2   Arundhati Roy, 'The Pandemic is a Portal', *Financial Times*, 3 April 2020. https://www.ft.com/content/10d8f5e8-74eb-11ea-95fe-fcd274e920ca; accessed on 1 January 2021.

3   Isabel Allende, *Island Beneath the Sea* (M. Sayers Peden, Trans.), London: Fourth Estate, 2010.

4   Quoted in Bridget Nicholls, 'How Cousteau Inspired My Love of the Oceans', BBC.com, 20 November 2010. https://www.bbc.com/news/world-11789975; accessed on 1 January 2021.

5   Rebecca Solnit, *Hope in the Dark*, Edinburgh: Canongate Books, 2004.

Life Goes On in Clarinbridge

A Reflection by John Quinn

In Toberbracken, Castlegar and Taramuid
Farming life is full steam ahead
Cows are milked and calves are fed
There's fertiliser to be spread.
And the grass is growing once again
'I think we could do with a drop of rain …'
Life goes on in Clarinbridge.

In Kileelybeg and Kileelymore
It's hard enough to keep the score.
Back-yard Cup Final – there's a wailing
      roar
Dad has let in another goal.
It's hard to play rugby with no ruck or maul

And a sliotar rebounds off the gable wall …
Life goes on in Clarinbridge.

In Dunkellin, Roveagh, Moyvilla West
Everyone's doing their level best.
A cycling family pass in Indian file
And greet the joggers with a smile.
Piano practice brings a certain pain
And someone's cheating at Ludo – again…
Life goes on in Clarinbridge.

In Cahirweelder, Ballinstaig and Rhynn
School is out – or is it in?
My God, what's that in the mayonnaise
jar?
It's my worm collection – I've thirteen so
far!
Ten long division sums? That's *unreal*!
No sums – No tree house. That's the deal!
Life goes on in Clarinbridge.

In Stradbally North, South and East
Life is just a non-stop feast.

There's a pot of stew – that will last three
    days! –
And next comes the rattle of baking trays
Who told my sister she's a baking master?
That banoffi pie was a complete disaster!
Life goes on in Clarinbridge.

In Slieveaun, Coolratty and Cloughlahard
They're living life with no holds barred.
Green-fingered gardeners are at their ease
While total novices plant beans and peas.
Somewhere a lawnmower stutters and stalls
(We can't print the owner's anguished
    calls …)
Life goes on in Clarinbridge.

In Kilcolgan and the 'Bridge itself
Centra and Londis are restocking shelf by
    shelf
The shops are busy – two metres – you know
    the score
There's a one-way system in James Kelly's
    store.

Wheaten flour's in short supply
But the toilet rolls are stacked up high …
Life goes on in Clarinbridge.

In Ballinamana, Gortard and Cave
They're chasing hobbies on the crest of a
    wave
At last 'himself' has painted the spare room
Must show it to the neighbours on Zoom!
Now he's surely lost the head – what do
    you think?
He's painting the shed in a shocking pink!
Life goes on in Clarinbridge.

In Hillpark, Kilcolgan, Ballinabucky
The TV addicts are feeling lucky.
Got the kids to bed at last – 'But it's not
    even dark!'
Now for the next episode of Ozark!
God, I'm dying for some real sport on telly
Oh no – not another re-run of Dublin v
    Kerry!
Life goes on in Clarinbridge.

Postscript

My wonderful neighbour Maureen O'Loan died from cancer on 11 July 2020. I wrote these lines in her memory.

For Maureen

A Reflection by John Quinn

Wife, mum, grandmum and more
With an abundance of love to share.
To a family that was so blessed
You poured out love like a prayer.

A true neighbour and dear friend
To cherish every day
You gave each of us your all

In your quiet gentle way.

Always a kindly gesture
Maybe a present to treasure.
No problem and no fuss
Giving was your pleasure.

How can we thank you enough
Except indeed to pray
That you now enjoy your great reward
In your quiet, gentle way.

List of Contributors

ROSS BEATON is a secondary school English teacher from Dublin. He studied in Mater Dei Institute of Education before completing his masters in Trinity College, Dublin. He is currently teaching in an international school in Abu Dhabi in the United Arab Emirates.

PETER BIRKINSHAW owns a small cleaning company in the West of Ireland. Having been drawn to explore the Catholic faith further, Peter has spent the last four years studying at the Priory Institute in Dublin, a Dominican centre for theological studies. Peter resides in County Galway with his wife Susan and two daughters Emily and Holly.

JOHN ED DESTEFANO, STB, M.Div., is currently retired. Ed has served the Church in multiple ministries for more than fifty years. Ed has served the catechetical mission of the Church full time since 1980. For the last eleven years Ed has been a member of the Veritas team that developed its *Credo* high school series.

NANCY MORRISON DESTEFANO, LCSW, MA Theology, is an ordained Methodist Elder who currently serves as Pastoral Minister at the Episcopal Church of the Transfiguration, Dallas, Texas. Nancy has served the people of God in various ministries for more than forty years.

MARIE DUNNE CHF is a native of Dublin and a member of the Congregation of the Sisters of the Holy Faith. Marie has a background in education and pastoral ministry and is a composer of both sacred and inspirational music. She has also been a choral director of choirs for many years. With faith at the core of Marie's music ministry, she endeavours to use life's experiences to reach and connect with others through her ministry.

GLENN GANNON is an actor, writer and homeless advocate. His writing includes his memoirs *Miracle Man: From Homeless to Hollywood* and plays *Tears of a Clown*, *Only Make Believe* and *The Trial*. He is a regular contributor to the American online magazine *Bellesprit* and is an ambassador for the Dublin Simon Community.

CLARE GILMORE is a native of the Ards Peninsula in Co. Down. She graduated from Milltown Institute of Theology and Philosophy in 2000 with a BA in Theology and Ministry and worked in a variety of ministries across Ireland, including in youth ministry, school chaplaincy, retreat teams and diocesan bodies, before deciding to focus on adult faith development. For the last number of years she has been very involved in Drumalis Retreat and Conference Centre, Larne; and currently works part-time with the Redemptorists on their novena and parish mission team.

MARTIN (JARLATH) GORMALLY is a ninety-eight-year-old man living in Sligo.

JOHN QUINN is writer and former RTÉ broadcaster. He has published several titles with Veritas including *Gratias: A Little Book of Gratitude* in 2018, *A Book of Beginnings* in 2019 and *Daily Wisdom (Léann An Lae)* in 2020.

MEGAN McKENNA, a New York native now living in New Mexico, works internationally with parishes, dioceses, religious orders and organisations. She is author of forty-nine books, including *The Book of the Poor* and *This Will Be Remembered of Her*, which won a Catholic Press Association award. McKenna is an Ambassador of Peace for Pax Christi USA. She teaches at many universities, colleges and pastoral institutes around the world and presently works training elders in First Nations communities and dioceses in Canada and the United States.

LINDA MINTO is a writer and mother of four. After losing her baby son to cot death some years back, Linda has devoted her life to offering words of comfort, love and hope to others through her meaningful greeting cards and product ranges. Her website is www.lindaminto.com.

FINTAN MONAHAN is Bishop of Killaloe and is based in Ennis, Co. Clare. He was ordained to the priesthood for the Archdiocese of Tuam in 1991. He published *A Perfect Peace: Newman, Saint For Our Time* on St John Henry Newman in 2019 and *Peace Smiles: Rediscovering Thomas Merton* in 2020.

STEPHEN MONAGHAN CM is a Vincentian Priest (Order of St Vincent de Paul). He is a former Chaplain to the Deaf Community in Ireland. For the past four years he has worked at the Ambo Lazarist Deaf School (ALDS) Ethiopia and ministering at the parish of St Justin de Jacobi's. He was instrumental in helping to establish the Deaf School which opened in 2012. For more information on the Deaf School, please visit www.alds.info.

ANNE NEYLON DC lives in the local community with the Daughters of Charity of St Vincent de

Paul in Ballyfermot. She currently works as a Primary Diocesan Advisor in the Archdiocese of Dublin. Sister Anne is a member of the writing team for the *Grow in Love* Religious Education Programme for Primary Schools.

MARY ANN PAPP is a Catholic woman, wife, mother and lay minister residing in Ireland for more than eight years. Originally from New Jersey USA, she was employed as a Facilitator of Student Retreats at the Emmaus Center in Swords, County Dublin.

TOMI REICHENTAL is best known through his autobiography, *I was a Boy in Belsen* and two documentaries, *Till The Tenth Generation* and *Close to Evil*. Tomi Reichental was born in 1935 in Slovakia. He was sent to Bergen-Belsen concentration camp in 1944. Tomi has lived in Dublin since 1959 and regularly talks to Irish schools about his wartime experiences.

MAURA WALSH OSsR was born in Galway to very nurturing parents, Mary and Patrick, where a seed of faith grew, went on to mature, got lost, returned and finally took root within the life-giving walls of the Redemptoristine nuns in Dublin.

ANDREW WATSON is a Presbyterian Minister who has served parishes in Counties Donegal, Down and Monaghan. He's married to Hazel and they have four grown-up children. Besides his passion for Christ and scripture his interests include music, gardening, archery and playing bass and bodhran in trad sessions.